ONE NEW DUDE
by
Jeff Zahorsky

Text copyright © 2013
Jeff Zahorsky
All Rights Reserved

All rights reserved. This book is protected by the copyright laws of the United States of America. This book may not be copied or reprinted for commercial gain or profit. The use of short quotations or occasional page copying for personal or group study is permitted and encouraged. Permission will be granted upon request. NoWayDude Press™

Scripture quotations marked "NASB" from the New American Standard Bible®, Copyright © 1960, 1962, 1963, 1968, 1971, 1972, 1973,
1975, 1977, 1995 by The Lockman Foundation
Used by permission. (www.Lockman.org)

Scripture quotations marked "ESV" are from The Holy Bible, English Standard Version® (ESV®), copyright © 2001 by Crossway, a publishing ministry of Good News Publishers. Used by permission. All rights reserved.

Scripture quotations marked "NIV" THE HOLY BIBLE, NEW INTERNATIONAL VERSION®, NIV® Copyright © 1973, 1978, 1984, 2011 by Biblica, Inc.™ Used by permission. All rights reserved worldwide.

Scripture quotations marked "ISV" from the Holy Bible: International Standard Version®. Copyright © 1996-2012 by The ISV Foundation. ALL RIGHTS RESERVED INTERNATIONALLY. Used by permission.

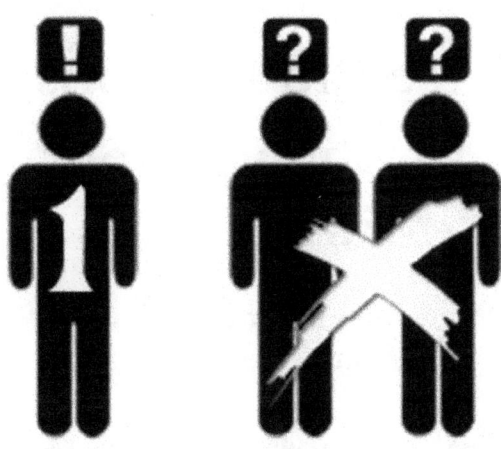

This book is dedicated to:
Jesus Christ
**Lord of lords, King of kings
Creator of Heaven & Earth
Thank You for sending Your Son, PaPa!**

"I love it. Everyone, this is a great book. A very real and appealing religious and theologically correct read for today's contemporary religiously pluralistic-oriented society. I highly recommend it. The author has done an excellent job. This is a must read."
— Professor Michael W. Langston, Seminary and School of Ministry at Columbia International University

7 Solid Reasons to Change Your Mind & Life!

Turning the Key on What God Says Resolves Your Ultimate Identity Crisis

The Bible describes this life we live on earth as a *vapor*. It's akin to some steam rising from a cup of hot coffee or tea, then—*poof!* It's gone. So fragile; so brief in light of eternity! Wouldn't it be a shame to get to the end of your life never having known who you really are? Of course it would be. This would be the ultimate oversight!

This book primarily addresses Christians but non-Christians are encouraged to read it, as well. Whether your life is in Christ or not, this book can be of tremendous value to you in this life—as well as the life to come. You may come to find it is very beneficial to know *who you actually are* in this existence we commonly refer to as *life*.

For those *not yet in Christ*, here are a few reasons why it's helpful to know your current & true identity.

Consequences. Being guilty before a holy God without a Savior has eternal consequences. God is a good Judge so He will judge all men on a fixed day—and He will righteously administer justice.

Direction. Knowing who you are today can help you to assess the direction you really want to go from here on in.

Justification. Receiving the Savior, Jesus Christ—by inviting Him into your heart for an eternally intimate relationship—will *justify* you before a holy God.

Glorification. Accepting the pardon in Christ allows for you to cross over from death into life, condemnation into justification. This ultimately climaxes into eternal glorification. We won't discuss all of those aspects within this book, but you should know: this *pardon*—this *salvation* along with all of its benefits—is available to you, today!

For those *in Christ*, here are *just a few* reasons why it's helpful to know your current and true identity.

> **God's Glory.** God is glorified in your life because the work He has done in you is more accurately and fully realized.
>
> **True Freedom.** You should no longer be left feeling confused, condemned, or ashamed. Understanding who you are is to realize Jesus suffered to take all of those burdens away from you.
>
> **Godliness.** You are more likely to behave in a way which is consistent with who you really are; a child of the Most High.
>
> **Victorious in Spiritual Warfare.** Settling the identity matter once and for all time encourages the casting down of arguments that contradict your true identity.

Quite surprisingly, I have come to discover that for years I have struggled with just exactly who I *really* am. Have you ever felt this way? It can be a bit troubling. Sounds like an identity crisis, doesn't it? I mean, how in the world can anyone lead an intentional, accurately informed and fulfilling life if they have yet to properly understand their true identity? Do you happen to realize the liabilities that come with this identity crisis?

If so, *then setting out to discover your true identity appears to be a reasonable objective, doesn't it?* Yes! I would agree! Therefore, let us begin our journey into this in-exhaustive, yet highly insightful topic of true identity. Christian or non-Christian, I invite you to be challenged and to think…again!

Tips for Reading This Book

You'll eventually notice this book is *pregnant*—on purpose. Since much needs to be examined regarding the topic of nature, Part 2 dominates most of the book. Let your *thinking* be pregnant with God's Word so you recognize who God says you truly are. All chapters lean on Holy Scripture in order to examine and establish who you truly are according to your Creator, God.

PART 1

Each chapter of this book is intended to encourage and exhort you. These first three chapters are no exception.

Chapter 1 lays the foundation. Chapters 2 and Chapter 3 serve as a *building up* to Part 2. Even though these chapters are relatively brief, the truth emphasized shouldn't be underestimated. The impact of the revelatory details is of eternal value, both in this life and the life to come!

PART 2

Chapter 4 is by far the largest chapter. *Expect plenty of extra emphasis regarding the sinful nature.* Since nature is directly related to your identity, much attention and detail is given to it. Put on your thinking *and* reasoning cap! You will be encouraged *multiple times* using various angles and Bible verses to uncover your true identity—as has been revealed by God. Prepare to think about who you *truly* are… again!

PART 3

Slide down the summit of the most involved chapter with an enjoyable landing into the final three chapters and Conclusion. In these chapters you will continue to receive *good news*. You will complete your inventory which examines God's revelation of your identity. From there, you can check out the *Resources & Links* section. Be blessed as you continue this magnificent journey. God has prepared *all of it ahead of time*—specifically for you!

Table of Contents

7 Solid Reasons to Change Your Mind & Life!

Turning the Key on What God Says Resolves Your Ultimate Identity Crisis 4

Tips for Reading This Book 6

PART 1

Chapter 1 15

PROJECT: Dude Inventory 15

- Why All the Confusion? 17
- Staying Open to God's Word 24
- Remain Open 25
- Inventory! 27

Chapter 2

PROJECT: Heart Inventory 30

- HeartLine 31
- The Promise 31
- A Proper Cut 33
- Summary 34
- Life Application 37

Chapter 3

PROJECT: 38

Mind Inventory 38

- Straight Up 38

Write Here 42
Summary 43
Life Application 46

PART 2
Chapter 4
PROJECT: Nature Inventory 48

The Holy Spirit Leads You to Truth 50
Varying Nature Viewpoints 52
Turning the Key 54
Absorbing Truth 58
Sinking Your Roots 60
Turning the Key Finds True Rest 64
Paul Turned the Key 71
"Father of Faith" Turned the Key 71
Esther & Mary Turned the Key 73
De-Terminator 77
Spiritual Condition 78
Re-Affirming Truth 81
Check Your Charge 85
The "Flesh" 88
In the Original 89
Humanness 91
Translations & Perspectives 95
Drawing Distinctions 97
Jesus Drew Distinctions 100
Flesh/Body = Weak 102
Jesus is Strong! 102

Nailing Down the Flesh	103
Got Buckets?	107
Accounting for Sin	110
Assigning Sin's Proper Place	113
You Lookin' at Me?	118
Come... Let Us Reason	124
Paul Beats Body - Not Old Self	126
Recurring Death?	126
Dirty Deeds	128
In This Corner!	130
Kaboom!	132
Sanctification Insights	136
Becoming You - Sanctification	140
Romans 7	144
The Scanning	145
Poof!	148
Your Response	154
You are Not in the Flesh	155
Your Divine Nature	156
Renewed in Knowledge	158
Truth or Consequences	160
Summary	162
The Sonsets Free!	166
Life Application	168

PART 3
Chapter 5
PROJECT:
Righteousness Inventory 171
- Rags to Riches 172
- Summary 176
- Life Application 178

Chapter 6
PROJECT: Spirit Inventory 179
- Breathe 180
- Marked 182
- Testing 183
- Summary 184
- Life Application 186

Chapter 7
PROJECT: Soul Inventory 187
- Got Soul? 187
- Catastrophic Coverage 189
- Summary 190
- Life Application 192

Conclusion 193
Resources & Links 200
About Jeff Zahorsky 201
Endnotes 202

PART 1

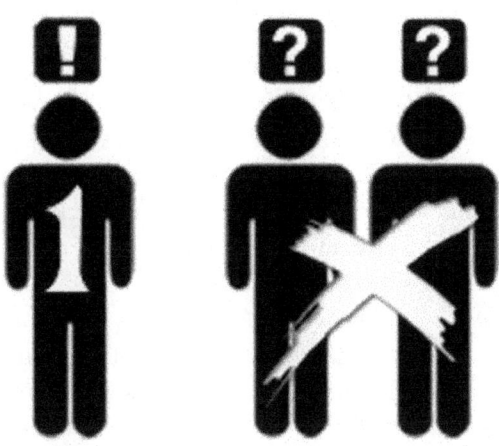

Chapter 1

PROJECT:
Dude Inventory

As I stared at my computer screen, I was speechless & stunned. It displayed the following:

> **"Those who belong to Christ Jesus have crucified the sinful nature with its passions and desires."**
> **~ Galatians 5:24 NIV**

"What in the world? *I have?*" I thought to myself. *"This does not describe me, and I <u>do</u> belong to Christ! Or, at least I thought I did?"* It was as if out of nowhere I was standing all alone. Nothing was in my universe except my eyeballs staring at those words. I sat not even knowing who I was for what seemed like a lifetime—but it was only seconds.

Horrific! How could I have overlooked this after all of this time in God's Word? Had I ever read this before? I *had* to have read it! What had I done then? Had I just moved past it hastily, chalking it up as another one of those, *"nice-thought-God-but-not-in-this-lifetime-that's-for-sure"* verses?

I thought I had done everything I needed to do! Sure, I knew it was not about me. Rather, it was all about Jesus and what *He* had done. Nevertheless, I was still compelled to examine my journey to this point. Let's see. I received Christ: check. I accepted and received his forgiveness; check. I followed Him daily; check. I resolved to resist temptation daily; check! I preached. I exhorted. I posted. I shared. Check, check, check, check.

Yet, *I could not believe my eyes!* This Bible verse was so succinct, so penetrating and so *unavoidable!* For the first time in my life I sensed in my spirit God stopping me at this particular verse. Since then, my understanding of who I truly am has never been the same.

Maybe you're like me. Perhaps? Maybe you have learned your entire Christian walk you are actually two different people; *two different natures*. A *good* you and a *bad* you. Dude, if you are supernaturally born from above and believing this to be true, let me share something with you: *you are missing out on God's abundance of grace, all designed specifically for you!* Please know I'm aware this is a contended subject. Even so, I'm here to tell you: God did not supernaturally re-create you into some split-personality being! This has to be stated right out of the gate. Not just once but multiple times! *"Repetition is the mother of learning."* I have heard it said. Therefore, please allow me to make sure I don't disappoint. Know this: You are *One New Dude*, Christian! *Uno!*

The Lord has given no indication in his Word He intends for you to perplexedly sojourn through this life as if you were some scattered, *partially* redeemed human being. No way! *You are One New Dude!* You are not two different people dwelling inside of one body! Isn't this good news?

As a new creation—a partaker in the divine nature—you are currently *confined* to your *not-yet-but-soon-to-be-redeemed body, or "flesh."* Now, this might sound a bit disconcerting at first blush. However, I'm here to tell you… it's a galaxy away from disconcerting! Once you benefit from its reality in your life you will likely never be the same. Why? Because you will begin to receive everything Jesus has done for you. At the moment of conversion, whether or not you *felt this*, *realized this*, or *none of the above*… Jesus supernaturally re-created you as *One New Dude*. It was supernatural!

Please begin to let this truth marinate throughout your being. By God's grace, the *real you* has been catapulted into existing as a partaker in the divine nature! Your *unredeemed flesh* is the body you will shed one of these days ahead—perhaps in the not-so-distant future. That is all; that is it! *One New Dude!* You exist as *one, unique, distinct* & <u>saved</u> individual thanks to your Savior & Lord, **Jesus Christ!** You have *one spirit, one heart, one mind, one nature, one righteousness & one soul.*

Critics may talk! Are you a people-pleaser or a God-pleaser? Are you still trying to please men? Of course you're not! You trust the Lord, ultimately! Am I right? So now, if you are willing to receive God's grace in full, you can walk in *true* newness of life. A newness of life you may well have never experienced before. It is my privilege to bring to you encouragement, standing upon the eternal Word of God entirely by God's grace, alone.

Why All the Confusion?

So, you might be saying to yourself: *"JZ, I'm really confused, now. I've never been taught what you're teaching. Are you really serious, 'Dude'?"*

I am serious, Dude! So, let me ask you this: How many times have you heard you have two *natures?* Can you even begin to count? I doubt you can! I certainly wouldn't be able to count for myself, either.

Christians are not in full agreement on this matter. One thing you can be sure of though is: your adversary Satan prowls like a roaring lion seeking whom he may devour. For you to walk in victory and authority spells more bad news for him. For you to actually take God at his Word causes Satan and his demons to tremble. They trembled in the presence of Jesus. If Jesus is in you they are not really excited about it!

Yes. Satan and demons are *real.* Hopefully, you already get this. Causing confusion within your mind is one last weak but clever attempt of the enemy to subdue you as a child of God. Satan doesn't want you to discover the truth about yourself. Are you kidding me? Satan wants to paralyze you in your new life, even if this *new life* has been for 20 or 40 years already. It suits your adversary just fine to suggest Jesus accomplished less for you than He actually did!

Consider this: Jesus goes ahead and does a bunch of mind-blowing, life-altering stuff for you at the cross. Then true-to-form, Satan twists scripture—just like he did in the Garden of Eden.

Satan's a liar. Satan will whisper, *"You aren't new. OK, maybe you're kind of new, but it's not guaranteed and there's a real good chance the old you is going to win out!"*

Satan wants to leave you confused, off-balance, and with a false sense of humility. The Liar doesn't want you fully embracing the *only covenant* belonging to you: the *New One!*

"Mix them together, instead. Do it intentionally or unintentionally; I don't care!" he hisses. *"Just make sure you reject the true Gospel of grace promised in the New Covenant. Stay in the Old Covenant! Replace pure grace with a watered-down version of what really happened at the Cross."*

Missing what God has for you would suit your enemy just fine. *Don't* walk in abundance. *Don't* release your God-given authority into the world being governed by the prince of the power of the air. *Recede. Shrink back.* Call yourself a *sinner* until you forget what a *son* is. Tell everyone how wicked you are and how you just can't wait to go be with Jesus instead of stomping out lies and hell, here and now.

How does this tragedy happen? It happens for at least a few reasons, I would propose. Perhaps you'd be willing to consider these reasons?

1. Awareness: Maybe you *have not been made aware* of specific, supernatural accomplishments of Christ at the cross—all for your *new life* benefit. He's a sacrificial, loving God, isn't He? He did not spare his only Son for you. You are precious to Him. You can see this as you observe the Cross of Calvary.

Interestingly enough, the earliest printed Bibles with Bible commentaries appear to have been used at seminaries. If these Bible commentaries side with a two-natured view over a one-natured view, is it any surprise the *sinful nature co-existing with a divine nature view* would be the dominant view in the Church today?

Know this: I love Christ. I love His Church. I love all of my brothers and sisters because love is a choice and Jesus lives in me. Martin Luther loved, as well. Paul loved. Jesus loved/loves. Yet, Bible truth has a way of shaking up popular views, doesn't it? Those in disagreement with the Gospel of grace *on any level* have historically considered themselves to be on the same side as God. As we have learned over time, this did not *always* secure a position actually on the side of God's Word. We have to be very careful we don't end up misunderstanding grace. Granted, the suggestions and exhortations of this book may fall short in a number of areas. At the same time, *holding to* and *never letting go of* what could be less than God's best is not to be applauded! Consider that which God has put before you and test it to see if He might not have more for you to discover!

2. Receiving: Maybe you *have been made aware* of the truth of what Jesus has done for you. However, perhaps you have yet to come to a place of *fully receiving all aspects of what* Christ has accomplished on your behalf. We'll try to uncover and point out what those particulars might be as we proceed through this book. I believe it will bless you.

3. Belief: Another reason might be there is a lack of *simple belief*. Uh, oh! This strikes me as the right time for an urgent disclaimer—*Urgent!*

Please understand this up front: my objective is *not* to attack the measure of faith God has given to you. I believe I have been called to exhort you. To comfort with the comfort I have received. Your faith is precious to God and without it—it's impossible to please Him. So, you need to keep what you have and build upon it. My goal is not to rob you of this because we all could stand to have our faith increased, amen? On the same note, I'm not here to tear you down. Rather, my desire is to build you up. With this clarified let's go ahead and continue towards the point. The point suggests the *possibility* of any one of us lacking *simple belief*, a *child-like faith*, in what God says.

I heard a sermon recently mentioning it's the *faith of Christ* that matters, not our own faith. It's an interesting angle. It's actually encouraging because we fall short but Jesus never does. In a very real sense, I have no issue with the idea of getting and keeping our eyes focused upon Jesus. He is always the answer, to be sure!

This conceded, you & I certainly *do participate* in our walk with God—exercising & activating the faith that has been given—do we not? For example, Jesus always seems to encourage people to *put legs* to their faith when He performs miracles, doesn't He? Remember when Peter *stepped out of the boat?* How about when Jesus asked the one guy, *"Do you want to be healed?"*[4] The man indicated he did desire to be made well, yet he made an appeal to Jesus he required assistance. When he did so, Jesus told him he was healed and to get up and walk. In both cases, legs were put to each person's faith.

This is precisely why the role we play in believing God or not believing God is so vital. God allows us to participate in his miracles & sovereign plan, *through faith in Him.* What a privilege! Don't forget: When Abraham believed God — when he took God at his Word and trusted what God said—he was made *right* with God. It was credited to him as *righteousness*; do you remember? This is a key takeaway, as we proceed through this discovery process.

"So, what about this point, JZ? Why are you laying such a long foundation and emphasizing this point so drastically?"

Incredibly, as has been the case in my life, perhaps you have been *glossing over* major revelations in Scripture? You may be reading them, but are you recognizing their significance and trusting what they say as Holy Spirit inspired text?

"JZ, why would you suggest I might have been and still may be 'glossing' over certain scriptures?"

Perhaps it's because I caught *myself* doing it. This doesn't necessitate you must be doing the same thing, but it never hurts to make sure, right?

Your identity hangs in the balance!

As I considered my own shortcomings, I wondered: *"Could I be the only one doing the math that doesn't match up with what I am reading?"* I mean… is it *that unlikely* as sheep we could, at times, *camp upon* and *settle* for just one view—even when there are more to consider? We never take the path of least resistance or settle into any comfort zones, do we? Let me be the first to admit it. I have done this more than once. I am certain of it! For those of us who might struggle at times, perplexedly shaking our head at certain scriptures—there is hope! You do not need to run back to verses which seem to infer *personal effort* or make *you* the focus any longer. *The Lord has taken the battle out of your hands.*

Here's a sampling of the types of verses I'm referring to:

> "I have been crucified with Christ; and it is no longer I who live, but Christ lives in me;"
> **~ Galatians 2:20 NIV**

Or—how about this one?

> "…*knowing this, that <u>our old self was crucified with Him</u>, in order that our body of sin might be done away with, so that we would no longer be slaves to sin.*"
> **~ Romans 6:6 NASB**

The past tense verses in the Bible about the *old self*—which include these verses—appear to be succinct and singled-out as opportunities for both you & me to activate our faith. They are there for us to trust the specific truths God is revealing to us, no matter how unbelievable they may seem. Is this not a reasonable conclusion, based upon the text? God is *breaking it down* for us, as it were. The job of the believer—which is you if you are saved—is to *believe;* isn't that right?

However, what can you and I so easily fall prey to? How about this, for example? Rather than focusing on the types of verses above—the ones revealing the *old self* is now dead—we get caught up in the war between the Spirit and the flesh. The flesh still possesses certain misdeeds of the *old self*. Those deeds would manifest in certain ugly acts or behaviors... were it not for the power of the Holy Spirit putting those deeds to death. In fact, just because one has the Holy Spirit does not insure He cannot be grieved and quenched. Instead, let it be the *vestiges* of the old self which *no longer breathe!* Knowing who you are as a new creation has its benefits. You are not to be a *divided, off-balanced* and *confused* new creation. This isn't Christ's plan for you. Be the new creation who is the *undivided, intentional and purposeful inner man!* This conversely causes your walk to take on a whole new experience, just as Jesus planned for you!

In any case, I would invite you to consider, in a certain sense—not all senses, but in a certain sense—these verses we sometimes focus upon do not immediately steady our minds upon what *Jesus has accomplished*. You & I can instead get caught up into who we once *were*, what we once *had*, as well as the remaining challenges of walking in faith.

When these deterrents and distractions cloud our vision to what's really going on and everything seems to pile on—one negative thought after another—you can easily find yourself off-balance and even discouraged. Almost instantly, the appropriate focus gets thrown out of kilter. *Warning! Warning! My focus is no longer on Jesus! It's one me!*

Christian, how were you saved? Were you saved by your own efforts, or by God's gift? What have you ever merited on your own before a holy God? We're all listening? Exactly! Nothing! *God has done it all in Christ!* I do understand. I do empathize. We like to work for things, even after we get saved, right? It's a trap! Don't buy into the hype!

Even still, we have to remain focused. We need to *major in the majors*. Regardless of the sin that remains in your unredeemed body, God has supernaturally re-created you if you have been born twice.

It's not about rejecting what God is telling us Christ has done. It's not about trying to win what Christ has already won. It's about taking God at his Word and sticking to the plan. It's about *receiving, not achieving!*

Granted, many of us are still getting used to being a *new creation* while we're still occupying this unredeemed body of ours. I'll raise my hand first on this. As a forgiven child of God, the new you—*the new dude*—wills to beat back its *unredeemed flesh*, or body. Your heart's desire now is it would *not* rule you as it once did. That was when you were *degenerate*, or *not-yet-regenerated* by the power of God's Holy Spirit. It's a terrific sign! It's consistent with a *regenerated* heart! Your body had gotten used to getting *what it wanted when it wanted it,* and this was oftentimes outside of God's boundaries. Isn't that right?

Sadly, concentrating on *self-effort* instead of what Jesus has accomplished and offers as a gift shifts the focus back to you, instead of remaining on Jesus. Your focus belongs on Christ. This is where it *must remain* in order for you to have the victory—relying completely upon Jesus!

Friend, I know enough from personal experience as to what it can be like to have an identity crisis. *Do not feel all alone!* If you think you still have an old man I'm making the exhortation to *you*. I'm on your team and so is the Lord! Jesus is bigger than any crisis we may face, amen? Amen!

Here's the eight-hundred pound gorilla in the room. As stated before, *critics may talk*. They may mean well and refer to the Bible for truth, and those with a different view mean well and refer to the Bible for truth, as well. For any critics, let's maintain our love for each other in the Spirit of Christ and establish some logic.

Either you have two natures or just one nature. If two natures existing in the believer is correct, then I (along with *legitimate* and otherwise seasoned expositors) am incorrect about what God has revealed.

On the other hand, if holding to a *double-natured* view is incorrect then those who oppose this view, including myself—and hopefully you after you read this book— are correct. Regardless, under no circumstance can both be right at the same time, in the same sense. This would be contradictory.

No matter what the outcome of your belief, we are all one body and love is what we are being conformed to as these matters are discussed. We're simply examining what Christ has done and given to us, as a gift. So long as it's discussed in love and to build up, we should be able to take a closer look at things without injuring each other.

Driving more closely to the point, many Christians *are in an identity crisis*. The stakes could not be higher as I see it. Let's make an observation. Fighting something or someone who has already been crucified and buried is like chasing a mirage! Your job—as well as mine—is to believe what God has said. It's the Word of God that converts the soul, is it not?

Why might you or other Christians think we have both an old nature and a new nature? Please allow me to take a stab at it, if I may.

Apart from how the facts have already been digested, could it be because it's been ingrained into your soul, over the years... week after week, month after month? Is it possible? No other view could possibly make sense?

Tragic my friend. Tragic! I couldn't be more fired up than I am this moment as I begin to share these amazing truths with you. It's about the Lord & what He has done for you! I've walked around confused and beating myself up for years. God's Spirit so moved me when He revealed this to me I had to tell you about it! I'm not even kidding! Once I received and trusted what God *said/says*, my life was transformed! A simple attitude adjustment does wonders in life, doesn't it? How much more when we adjust our attitude to *line up in faith* with the living God! He is good! Without faith it is impossible to please Him and He is a *Rewarder* of those who diligently seek Him. Not *casually* seek Him. *Diligently* seek *Him,* like: "Jesus... what did You *really* do for me, at the cross? I want to know!" Something like that; *diligently!*

Everybody has an opinion, but the Holy Spirit says to you today: *"I tell you the truth!"* Two teachers or believers may have a different *take* on what has been revealed to us by God, in the Bible. As you consider the differing views seek the Holy Spirit and He will guide you to the right answer.[2]

With that said, hold onto your seat *because it is on now!* In investigating, *"One New Dude"* you have officially been placed *on notice!* You will now need a different *bucket* to account for the reason why you still are capable of committing sin. You will come to discover your *usual bucket* is no longer available. It will be akin to having a security blanket torn away from you. What will you do now? How will you view yourself and your Savior? Are you ready for it? *Let's hope so!* This brief time you have to walk by faith and receive God's promises is ticking away. The Spirit of God encourages us: *"Out with the old and in with the new!"*

Staying Open to God's Word

As we move forward, some quick questions for you beforehand:
If Jesus accomplished something on your behalf and you have not been made fully aware of it, would this be valuable information to you? Is it worth discovering and then receiving?

Are you prepared to be a recipient of *all* of God's grace?

Is there any chance you could be rejecting a certain portion of *grace*, intentionally or unintentionally?

Let's say on this broader issue of grace you are simply unsure. We all experience times of uncertainty; this is common. Yet, when it comes to this matter of grace, how important is it we continue to let God open our eyes? We don't see everything at once usually, right? Oftentimes, it *takes some time* to put things together. I would offer this is one of those cases. The case of your identity as it relates to what your Savior has accomplished for you. We want to see and know as much of what He has done and what He is offering, *don't we?*

Be encouraged to remain open to reasonable scriptural viewpoints, even if those viewpoints don't automatically match up with your current, comfortable position. You can do so without allowing me—or anyone else for that matter—to take you for a ride. If you *have* been studying your Bible then you likely have enough of a *root system* in place to at least entertain varying viewpoints held by other Christians. We know ultimately the Lord wrote the book. It's the Lord who's going to counsel you as you seek Him. You can't go wrong if you trust in the Lord!

In any case, that's how absolutely astonishing this matter of identity is to me, now. Like you may be right now I found myself, *unsure*. By the way, there's nothing wrong with asking questions. *"Just be prepared to accept the answers!"* is what I have learned. Being *unsure* is where it all started for me. It was a place of no longer being *certain* when I thought something was certainly certain; *my identity!*

As it turns out, I was missing God on this critical matter of identity. I was *glossing over verses* Jesus was serious about me *accepting*... and He still is. This is why we keep reading God's Word, amen? If it doesn't all compute the first or even the fiftieth time—or if some things are just too hard to believe at the onset—God is patient towards you!

I caught myself sitting in bewilderment when reading from Galatians 5:24. *It stared me right in the face and I had no answer for it.* Everything stopped for me. The words in this verse no longer permitted me to ignore them. They were not matching up and I was *utterly befuddled!*

My choice as I saw it was two-fold:

1. **Blow it off.** *Don't change your mind. In other words, don't repent.* Proceed forward, even if it means *"Do not pass Go!"* on God's promises for me.

2. **Do not** **blow it off:** *Do change your mind. In other words, do repent.* Take God at his Word, and then… proceed. *"Pass Go!"* Receive all the Savior has done. Intentionally walk as the true new creation God has created.

I chose the latter which is a big reason why we're here. *Hallelujah!*

Remain Open

Dude, this is *your identity* now… being discussed. I've heard it said sometimes people can be so open-minded their brains fall out! I'm not asking you to do this. Receiving what God has gifted to you with *palms up* in no way requires you to discount co-existing truths of scripture. As believers we still do have indwelling sin. There *is* a battle going on.

However, the specifics surrounding the battle with sin—along with convenient categories or *buckets* oftentimes adopted—may not always be consistent with scripture. I want to avoid this inconsistency, don't you? This is why I point you to much more exhaustive and edifying studies later on, in the *Resources* section.

In this book, the goal is much more to exhort and encourage you in Christ than it is to deal with every aspect concerning this supernatural work of God, in a true believer. We will get in depth to a certain degree. Yet, it's not as thorough and comprehensive as would be necessary to respond to every respected theologian or Christian who differs in their view.

Nevertheless, we are discussing your true identity in the midst of an invisible war where everything counts. These matters are not trivial!

If you know a lot about grace, then more re-enforcement certainly isn't going to hurt. If you're still seeking to better understand the magnitude of God's grace, then what you consider in this book—as it relates to scripture—*definitely* will not hurt you. This isn't any attempt to add any books to the Bible, either. It's *not*, "... *the Bible—plus this book*", as in the cults of the enemy's army. This book asks each reader to take a closer look at specific scriptures that hold the key to your identity.

God offers to each of us this amazing thing called *repentance* as you probably already know. Repentance is not about crawling on broken pieces of glass to earn God's favor, nor is it about performing certain religious rituals, right? It's about *changing your mind*. You thought one way about something, but then you decided it made better sense to change your mind about the thing. You are quite possibly already aware of this because you experienced it if/when you came to Christ. You thought one way about your lifestyle and position before God—but then, God showed you the truth and you changed your mind—isn't that right?

Now, this same reasoning applies to you as a blood bought child of God. If walking in truth always had to do with the most popular view, or getting everybody's approval, you would have never come this far, now would you have?

In this little journey, we're going to take inventory of not only the things Jesus has done for you, but you will also be challenged by the Spirit of God. This is because we'll continue referring to the Word and it *will challenge* you and change you. God will challenge you to *receive and to keep receiving!* How you currently view such revelation will serve to be a good indicator as to where you are in your faith walk. You have every reason to get excited if you are not, already!

This is a pursuit of *identity discovery*. We're going to have an inexhaustive—yet, in my opinion—an eternally insightful & eye-opening journey. It will be a journey into certain highlights and even some specifics of what God has revealed and wants you to know. God wants you to discover all He has done on your behalf, in Christ. Not just the things you already may know, but to have a deeper and more solid awareness of those things. That you would have a fresh, new understanding of God's goodness as it relates to who you are. This is about the *new you* Jesus has supernaturally created within the decaying yet soon-to-be-redeemed vessel you occupy, called a body.

When you say to yourself, *"God is good!"* you will hopefully agree with me, "That ain't the half of it! *Jesus is amazing!" He also thinks you are amazing!*

With this, if you have good reason(s) to change your mind about a thing we explore—perhaps even something you've held onto for a very long time—then by all means: accept God's gift of repentance, and... *change your mind!* It's ok to change your mind! Truly humble people change their mind when it makes good sense to have a change of mind.

You don't have to have each and every answer; I certainly don't. But let me remind you once more: Don't trade what God has said clearly for those things which may not be so clear in scripture. Remember this exhortation, as you proceed through this book. Think as you stand upon God's Word and as you depend upon and ask the Holy Spirit to illumine your mind. The One who created you is happy to tell you *in what ways* He has re-*created* you!

Inventory!

Rather than trade *what we know* for *what we don't know*, maybe it's time we take inventory? Why don't we begin to explore or even *re-explore* some of the highlights the Lord has promised to you and accomplished for you, already!

It occurred about 2,000 years ago—way back when Jesus Christ paid your sin penalty on the cross. If Jesus is your Savior and

Lord, you have a lot to be excited about. If Jesus is not your Savior and Lord as of yet, then you too can gain a better understanding of what there is to get so excited about, in Jesus. Your Creator is madly in love with you! He places tremendous value upon you as a living soul. He has amazing things in store for you if you'll seek Him and trust Him. He wants you in the family of God. This is why He sent His Son!

Coming up in the ensuing chapters we will:

> **Explore what God says about your Heart.** Since you have accepted Jesus, what does God say about your heart, now? How many hearts do you have, anyways? Can you clarify for me, God? Yes. *He can, He has and He will!*
> **Explore what God says about your Mind.** What revelation has God given to you about your mind? How many minds do you have? Does it matter what I think about what's going on in my head? *It matters, Dude!* God wants you to have your head on straight and He's given you just what you need to do it.

Oh, we're not done yet, Dude. We're just getting started! We will also:

> **Explore what God says about your Nature.** So much to cover, here! Who are you? God knows, and He's gonna tell you! He's already told you, but maybe we need to dig a bit deeper. Shall we? Let's knock down the walls and clear out all of the clutter in this mammoth chapter as God opens your eyes to the real you!
> **Explore what God says about your Righteousness.** Oh, you were not planning on standing before God on Judgment Day, all on your own, were you? Of course not! This is why you came to Jesus, right? Never again focus on your performance before God. Only believe! Only trust! See what God does with it.
> **Explore what God says about your Spirit.** Could God's revelation about your spirit be any more crucial to your identity? Tell me you said, *"No."* No way, Dude! It can't

be any more crucial! God's going to drive home more eternal truth to help you stay on point. Since God is Spirit, you can bank on your spirit playing a critical role, in your identity and relationship with your Creator. God doesn't want you confused. He wants you to walk intentionally, alive and seeing in true color!

Explore what God says about your Soul. What's a good way to understand your soul? Is your soul temporary or eternal? Where did your soul come from? Are you the owner of your soul? We'll take a brief look at what you've got as well as some other helpful information God provides for you.

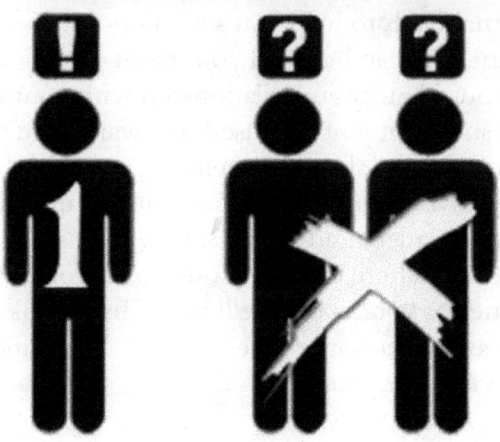

Chapter 2

PROJECT:
Heart Inventory

It's time to take inventory of your heart's situation as *One New Dude*. We're going to examine, in general, what this heart is you have. Let's look into what you had and what you now have. Why is it so important when we investigate the heart? If you are asking this, it's a reasonable question and you will want to be established in the awareness of what Jesus has done for you, regarding your heart.

This is not going to be a long chapter, but it should be sufficient in providing you with either new information or information you are familiar with, perhaps from another angle.

Either way or in another way, allow for it to re-enforce who you are in Jesus and praise God for all He has done and continues to do for you. Oh, what an amazing Creator we have. He certainly thinks you are worth all He has given and is giving.

HeartLine

"The eyes of the LORD search the whole earth in order to strengthen those whose hearts are fully committed to him."
~ 2 Chronicles 16:9 NLT

When we talk about the *heart* of the *One New Dude*, we're not talking about the physical organ. We're talking about the spiritual part of us that involves our emotions and desires.³ Some refer to the heart as the *center of our emotions*.

As an unsaved soul, you may have never asked yourself the question, *"How many hearts do I have?"* You may have even thought you had a good heart. Hopefully, by now and as *One New Dude* you realized you needed a heart *transplant*.⁴ It's the Christian who comes to learn and understands the heart is *deceitful* and *desperately wicked*,⁵ at least enough to seek and *surrender* to a Savior!

What's more, wasn't it incredible news when you came to learn God was giving out new hearts? *Shew!* That's some serious merchandise right there! You can't go down to the corner store, the Internet, or even the best physicians *on this planet* to get the kind of heart God's handing out.

Conversely, souls who have not called out to Jesus to save them yet typically think it's a good thing to *"follow your heart."* Yikes! Isn't this what the world system pumps into unsuspecting eyes and ears throughout the day? A heart that is deceitful and desperately wicked; you're going to follow it? Say it isn't so!

The Promise

JESUS SPEAKS: "For from within, out of the heart of man, come evil thoughts, sexual immorality, theft, murder, adultery, 22 coveting, wickedness, deceit, sensuality, envy, slander, pride, foolishness. All these evil things come from within, and they defile a person."
~ Mark 7:21–23 ESV

Nevertheless, we all know what it's like to follow our heart as an unsaved individual. Until we were born from above this is all we knew. We were slaves to sin and leaned upon our own understanding instead of trusting Jesus. Isn't God awesome? He is so patient with us and not willing any should spend eternity without Him. He was and is waiting to give those who would come to Christ a new heart. Let's look together at his promise:

> *"And I will give them <u>one heart</u>, and a new spirit I will put within them. I will remove the heart of stone from their flesh and give them a heart of flesh,"*
> **~ Ezekiel 11:19 ESV**

Is this not exciting, Dude? When you consider this for what it is, it's the miracle you needed! Before Jesus made you *One New Dude*, your heart was like a rock when it came to God or anything to do with what He says. This can lead to a lot of trouble both in this life and the one to come— to be sure! Imagine that. Not having a tender-loving heart towards God and expecting you'd obey Him or have relationship with Him. No way! The rock-hard heart isn't going to do it! Then you die and face judgment? No thank you! *"Where's the heart you're giving out Lord?"* right?

Exactly. So, Jesus saved you and God gave you the new heart. Since you and I were blinded to this stony heart by the cancer of sin, God had to reveal not only your old heart was stony, but your new heart is tender. A tender heart of flesh. *Ahh… much better.*

A love relationship with God through your Savior, Jesus Christ. Not a small thing to have this heart transplant! A heart that desires God rather than one that avoids Him. A heart that transforms you into a truly new creation. A heart that is the opposite of what you previously had. Stony to soft.

In other words, instead of not doing God's will, your heart is to do God's will. Instead of desires outside of God's boundaries, God gives you desires to obey his boundaries. God knows the secrets of the heart[6] and is also fully capable of changing your heart when you came to Jesus for help! God's the Giver, so this is of no surprise. Remember when Isaiah said he had unclean lips and God allowed for a spiritual being to fly to him and cleanse him by touching his mouth? Is there anything too hard for the Lord,[7] whether it's unclean lips or a stony heart?

"Then one of the seraphim flew to me, having in his hand a burning coal that he

had taken with tongs from the altar. And he touched my mouth and said: 'Behold, this has touched your lips; your guilt is taken away, and your sin atoned for.'"
~ **Isaiah 6:6-7**

This new heart is a gift only Jesus can offer to you because it was Jesus who shed his blood to establish the new covenant you're under. If you are confused about the state of your heart— perhaps because you experience some negative things surface at times—don't fall back into guilt, shame, the Law and the old covenant. That covenant *does not belong to you.*

Instead, grab hold of what God has done for you under the new and everlasting covenant. You get a new heart with this one. It's an amazing deal. As with anything else coming from God, you are to trust what God is saying is perfectly accurate. Your heart has been circumcised by God and his grace, in Christ.

A Proper Cut

As you proceed through this book and we discuss the various elements that headline each chapter, understand this *new heart* is right *at the heart of it!* Keep in mind and feel free to link this new heart with your divine nature. It's the circumcision of your heart that coincides with the work of the Holy Spirit and your true identity.

You have a lot to be excited about being born of the Spirit. God circumcised your heart. Many people have not experienced this, so we need to keep praying for them. Notice how religious people are always following their stony and deceitful hearts rather than getting a new one from Jesus. This causes legal issues when attempting to be justified before a holy and just God because the stony heart is hostile towards God. This heart does not walk in faith and without the *trust* component and a spiritual rebirth—the only thing remaining is condemnation. God justifies based upon faith in Christ, which is *trust*.

As *One New Dude*, you are not in the same sinking boat as the religious person or atheist. You came to Jesus broken and He did all the work. It's always been *more* about the inward condition of the heart than the external rituals with God. God wants your heart and when you gave him your old one, He traded it in for a new one. *Hallelujah!*

> *"For circumcision indeed is of value if you obey the law, but if you break the law, your circumcision becomes uncircumcision. So, if a man who is uncircumcised keeps the precepts of the law, will not his uncircumcision be regarded as circumcision? Then he who is physically uncircumcised but keeps the law will condemn you who have the written code and circumcision but break the law. For no one is a Jew who is merely one outwardly, nor is circumcision outward and physical. But a Jew is one inwardly, and circumcision is a matter of the heart, by the Spirit, not by the letter. His praise is not from man but from God."*
> **~ Romans 2:25-29 ESV**

Additionally, in the coming chapter's nature inventory, please take special note when you observe the highlighting of **Colossians 2:11**. This verse and passage in the Bible is directly related and *central* to your old, stony heart and your new heart of flesh. *Amazing stuff! Miraculous! All praise and glory to Jesus!*

Summary

Now that you are established in what Christ has provided for you under the new covenant, it's important to proceed along your journey in confidence. Due to this new heart God gave to you, your confidence is in Jesus and God's grace, alone. Like every other good thing and perfect gift, your new heart is a work of God.

Remember: the old heart of stone has been *replaced* with *one* new heart of flesh. It's God's truth and another opportunity for you to trust God with what He says. The old, deceitful, stony heart you had as a degenerate no longer applies. Christ has made all things new. He took out your old heart and put a new one in there. You no longer need to claim a deceitful heart because it's not part of the new covenant.

Sure, as we'll discuss in the *nature inventory* chapter, you are experiencing changes and growth as a result of your conversion. Yet, this does not change the facts regarding God's grace and the gift of this new *heart of flesh*. As you walk in faith you are led by the Spirit.

Your new heart is submissive to God; a stony and rebellious heart is not.

Speaking the truth against lies is what you are commanded to do! It's what Jesus did and He's your model for living. As you cast down arguments that exalt themselves against the knowledge of God, particularly regarding the condition of your heart—be encouraged! You have permission to grab hold of God's amazing grace which comes in the form of a new heart! You have relationship with the Father, through Jesus. You have a heart which loves God and desires to live for the Gospel. Your new heart prays and reads the Bible. Your new heart is devoted to Christ. The heart that did not identify with these things is gone!

If you've doubted this, *change your mind! It's that easy!* God said it, you now trust it. It's all good because God is in control! He does what He wills and by grace, He gave you a new heart that is responsive to Him. *Nurture* that! Guard your heart! Feed your heart continually with the truth of God's Word, the Bible.

Finally, this wasn't previously mentioned but *it is* critical to your relationships. If you haven't discovered this yet, you should know this new heart God gave you is *faithful* not only outwardly, but inwardly, as well.

"Neither circumcision nor uncircumcision means anything; <u>what counts is a new creation.</u>
~ Galatians 6:15 NIV

When we make mention of your physical body shortly, you need to know and always remember: your body no longer dictates and decides what's *going to go down* when faced with temptation. God gave you a new heart that not only impacts your relationship with Him in a positive way, but it also impacts your spouse, if you are married.

When you tally up all God has bestowed upon you in Christ—you will see or be reminded of once more—you have the power to do what is right. This is *true* freedom. Those who are not born-again do not have the freedom they *claim* to have. *"Why is that?"* you might ask? It's because they are actually in bondage. They *are not free to do what is right before God* because they don't possess this new heart! They have yet to come to Jesus to receive it at the foot of the cross. As *One New Dude* you have this new heart; we just took inventory. This gives you every reason to be joyful! God is good!

Why should you change your mind & your life?
Solid Reason #1:
You have One New Heart!

Ask, Seek, Knock.
Stop doubting and believe!

Life Application

1. Have you come to Jesus for your new heart?

2. As *One New Dude*, do you affirm this truth of God to yourself? Or, do you consider your heart the same old heart you had before Jesus?

3. What changes might you make to align yourself with God's truth?

PERSONAL NOTES

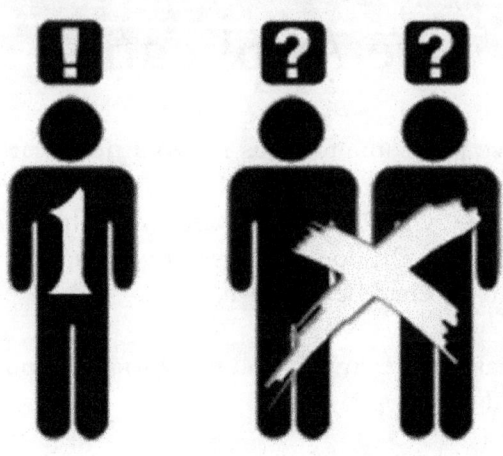

Chapter 3

PROJECT:

Mind Inventory

Let's jump right into this next inventory to examine briefly a general idea of *what the mind is* and what God says about the mind He gave to you, as *One New Dude*. There's a lot to celebrate here, too!

Straight Up

What is your mind? One simple definition might be, *"the sum of all thoughts."*[8] Also, if your heart is the center of your emotions, then the *mind* is the *center of the intellect*.

However you slice and dice it, do you realize as *One New Dude* you have been given a *new* mind? It's true! God is mega-famous for giving *all things* good and *this thing* most certainly is not absent from the list!

> *"For who has known the mind of the Lord that he may instruct him?*
> *But we have the mind of Christ."*
> **~ 1 Corinthians 2:16 ESV**

Would you agree you and I certainly will never instruct the Lord? Would you like to hear the astounding news again, though? Allow me the privilege. You—*One New Dude*—have the *mind of Christ*. You might say, *"Huh? Excuse me?"*

Yes, my brother in Jesus! God has given you amazing insight as his blood-bought child. It is because before your rebirth from above you did not share in God's *plan, purpose or perspective*.[9] This all changed when the Holy Spirit regenerated you, though. This new mind came pre-programmed![10]

First off, you do share in these supernatural things of God with this mind of Christ. You *do know* God's plan for the world. He is not willing any should spend forever without Him, for example. You get this now and you realize saving faith is required.

Secondly, just as Jesus came to seek and save the lost, so do you now have this mindset as you share the Good News. That's straight from Christ. You need to be informed and reminded of this, consistently. You have the mind of Christ!

Third, your perspective has changed. This is all supernatural and how many times do we gloss over what's actually going on in our lives, in Christ? Let it not be so! Understand as Christ was filled with, empowered by and led by the Spirit, so now are you! When you pray and depend upon God in your surrendered life, it is *straight up* the mind of Christ!

What about some more evidence for this new mind? Interestingly enough, the Lord uses revelation which points to the cancer of sin to simultaneously confirm your new mind. Consider what God reveals to us through Paul, in Romans 7:

> *"but I see another law at work in the members of my body, waging war against the law of my mind"*
> **~ Romans 7:23a NIV**

If you are the old dude with the old mind, another law wouldn't be waging war with the law of God—or the law of your mind—which is what Paul is expressing to be the case. Later in Romans 8, God reveals the *carnal mind is hostile towards God.*[11] This is good news for you as *One New Dude!* To identify with what Paul is saying is to recognize the law at work in the members of your body is not in your inner man, but rather your outer man; your *unredeemed humanness.*[12]

This new mind of yours is a mind which desires to do the will of the Father. The old nature you used to have did not have the mind of Christ, but rather a carnal mind. The carnal mind didn't desire to please God and it was unable to do so, regardless. That mind was focused on sinning, but your new mind of Christ is interested in the Lord Jesus and desires to please God. *Hallelujah!*

Seriously. I can promise you I would not be writing this book had God not given me the mind of Christ. This is not where I would be. It's a fact. What gets into a person that would cause them to write a book such as this one? It's simple: the Holy Ghost and the mind of Christ, Dude! He gave it to you too as *One New Dude!*

God isn't playing games. You and I need to catch up to and stay right where God wants us to be. None of this stuff where you read, *"We (you) have the mind of Christ"* then just going about your business like God didn't give you a new mind. That's not in the same category as faith. It's not about trusting what God says. If you didn't know it, that's OK. Now you do know it because God has revealed it for you to know. This is an exciting thing! Can we get an *"Amen!"* up in here?

It's to your advantage to get on board with this plan, if you aren't already. God designed it specifically for you! He knows about *every hair on your head.* We read:

*J*ESUS SPEAKS: *"Are not five sparrows sold for two pennies? Yet not one of them is forgotten by God. Indeed, <u>the very hairs of your head are all numbered.</u> Don't be afraid; you are worth more than many sparrows."*
~ Luke 12:6-7 NIV

If God knows the number of hairs on your head, what else do you think God knows about? God knows what *kind of mind* you have. He's the Creator and Redeemer. He's telling you what's going on with this new mind of Christ He has given you. It's not like the creature needs to tell the Creator what's going on, right? The Creator *reveals* to the creation *what's going on. He* calls the shots. *He* did the work. *He* reveals truth. *Lord, You are amazing!* Go ahead and tell Him, *One New Dude*. You know He's worthy! Let's praise Him, together!

Think about it. *"Where You go I also go, Jesus!"* That's not your *old mind* thinking, is it? You constantly death-walked, enslaved by sin before Jesus, did you not? That's not the mind of Christ. But God gave you the mind of Christ when you received Him, as we have learned. Don't ever put yourself down from this point forward. *Humility* doesn't disown what you have and who you are, in Jesus. It would actually be *prideful* to do such a thing.

You're new, Dude. You thought it was just an altar call which led to attending church, then doing some Bible study and treat your neighbors nicely, did you? You have your rapture shoes on, just holding on—hoping you don't slip up in the meantime?

Dude! You have the mind of Christ! Jesus broke sin's power over you. You are a child of God. You have a bunch of new invisible stuff ... straight from your Heavenly Father! It's like Christmas, Dude! He's made it so these invisible *gifts* are made manifest in your life! I'm not even talking about *spiritual gifts*—which is an entirely different, astonishing and supernatural subject.

I'm talking about what we're discussing, here. This book is an attempt to highlight what God has already made available to you, in the Bible. It's like you're sitting under the tree and God's gifts keep coming!

"What? You did what, Jesus? Oh? And you gave me this, too, Lord? Are You sure? I can't believe it." Believe it, Dude! You may have thought you believed but by the end of this book you might just be surprised. Dude, it's time for some serious belief. I'm not even trying fool with your mind of Christ.

That's right, Dude! You might be a bit awestruck just *considering* this mind thing. I can identify with that! Do you realize how much love God has lavished upon you? It's astonishing! We're talking about the Creator of the Universe, here. God owns all souls. He's the Master Designer. He's not tired. God *busts out* supernatural miracles of new creation every time a person accepts Christ. Not discovering, appreciating and enjoying all of his gifts is perhaps akin to leaving a stack of presents with your name under the Christmas tree.

It's like leaving those presents there and letting the garbage truck scoop them up because nobody wanted them. Don't let it happen, Dude! Life is a vapor. You know this. Jesus has you covered and you need to embrace all of these new covenant gifts. Out with the old! *You aren't Jeremiah, OK?* You aren't Job. Those awesome men of God were not under the new covenant— but you are! The covenant belonging to you is the *new one* and it has a lot of neat gifts in it. Know it!

Write Here

"This is the new covenant I will make with my people on that day, says the LORD: I will put my laws in their hearts, and I will write them on their minds."
~ Hebrews 10:16 NLT

"…will write my laws on their minds." more specifically, *your mind.* That's the mind of Christ!

You might find yourself saying, *"My old mind must still be there, because it still throws unwanted garbage up to me, all of the darn time!"* Let's just say for sake of argument your old mind is still there. Where do we put the thing? Is there room to fit them both inside of your head; an *old mind* and a *new mind?*

Realizing there may be plenty of room to fit both and more in certain cases, that's not the answer. It's not the child of God. The old is gone and the new has come. You have the mind of Christ. *Hallelujah!*

Some, I have heard it said, make a case for having two minds. Perhaps they believe the mind of Christ is the Holy Spirit who indwells the *One New Dude*. I wouldn't argue with this as it sounds *spot on.* You will also see the mind introduced in another explanation as you proceed. If the mind were a simple matter to explain, Christians would never have differing explanations for it. Yet, because the mind *is* a complex discussion, what I encourage you to do is hold onto what you *do know* and don't sacrifice it for what *you do not know!*

In the case of the *One New Dude*, we have established you have the mind of Christ. It comes across pretty straight forward in scripture. If you build upon this a few more things, you should be encouraged to consider you do *indeed* have one mind.

If it were not so, you'd have to ask yourself: does God desire ambivalence? Does God desire for all of his children to be ambivalent? What about the heart, soul, spirit and nature? Are those intended to be divided within God's new creation?

Allow me to invite you to consider this. God desires for you to be single-hearted *& single-minded*. First for Him—then also for your spouse, if you're married. Why would God want for you to have *more* than one mind? Is this why He gave you the mind of Christ—to have a divided mind? *No way, my friend!*

Check out a few of the verses God has for his children.

"That ye may with <u>one mind</u> and one mouth glorify God, even the Father of our Lord Jesus Christ."
~ Romans 15:6 KJV

"Finally, brothers, good-by. Aim for perfection, listen to my appeal, <u>be of one mind</u>, live in peace. And the God of love and peace will be with you."
~ 2 Corinthians 13:11 NIV

"complete my joy by being of the same mind, having the same love, being in full accord and <u>of one mind</u>."
~ Philippians 2:2 ESV

"Finally, all of you should <u>be of one mind</u>. Sympathize with each other. Love each other as brothers and sisters. Be tenderhearted, and keep a humble attitude."
~ 1 Peter 3:8 NLT

Summary

"BE OF ONE MIND" - why? Because God has given instruction in multiple ways and multiple times to be of one mind. God is interested in you being single-minded, not double-minded. You are *One New Dude!*

If you release your faith by *being of one mind* as instructed by your Creator, you align yourself with his supernatural plan for your life. Jesus is of *one mind* and under the new covenant; God gave you Christ's mind! You share in God's plan, purpose and perspective. It's a work of God. You have the mind of Christ. Can you believe this? You can believe it because God has given you the faith to do so!

Why should you change your mind & your life?
Solid Reason #2:
You have One New Mind!

Ask, Seek, Knock.
Stop doubting and believe!

Life Application

1. Have you come to Jesus for your new mind?

2. As *One New Dude*, do you *affirm* this truth of God to yourself? Or, do you consider your mind the same old mind you had before Jesus?

3. What changes might you make to align yourself with God's truth?

PERSONAL NOTES

PART 2

Chapter 4

PROJECT:
Nature Inventory

"And no one puts new wine into old wineskins. For the new wine would burst the wineskins, spilling the wine and ruining the skins."
~ Luke 5:37 NLT

As one who trusts in Christ, God has given you a gift that has crucified your sinful nature and by rebirth, has caused you to become a partaker of the divine nature. This is a miracle. *It's supernatural!*

Accordingly, let's consider several things as we investigate what God says about you. First though, allow me to give you some personal background and perspective as I've made observations within the body of Christ. These observations are made with a sincere desire to seek the Lord and truth. Jesus directed us to *"Ask, seek and knock."* Investigating and discovering together allows for the mutual benefits and blessings that are ultimately realized. So, let's take advantage of this and enjoy the journey!

Setting out, we'll consider a few personal observations which will hopefully be of tremendous benefit to you. You will also be encouraged and exhorted to let God guide you into the truth with regard to who you truly are! This will all be accentuated with multiple glimpses of related scriptures, exhortations, some terminology investigation, several *allocation* illustrations *("Where does everything go?")*, as well as several points that attempt to clarify and satisfy, with regard to the possibility of a sinful nature still being *alive* or even *operative*.

By the way, keep in the front of your mind something as you continue forward. The steady dose of challenges and exhortations with regard to the phrase, *sinful nature* is offered with an important distinction which should be made up front.

For the purposes of encouraging you in the area of true identity, the phrase *sinful nature* is being equated to your *old self* only; not with your *physical body*. It's been my experience the moment a Bible teacher (or even another Christian) refers to the *sinful nature*; they oftentimes reveal they are *not* convinced it is crucified. Attaching phrases akin to, *"The old man rising up…"* many Christians are left entirely off balance on this critical matter of identity. Rather than becoming *more* persuaded of the *One New Dude* God has created, Christians can become *less* certain. Fear and dread of the *old dude* coming back from the grave, as it were, clouds the mind. Brothers and sisters, this should not be so!

While this idea might sound entertaining and perhaps even fascinating to us—as if it's some type of real life *horror thriller*—it runs into problems with other scriptures which have been highlighted for you within this book. These succinct verses *do require a response*. It's always easier to say one believes what God says than to actually believe or *trust* what God says. You will likely understand this point much more clearly as you move deeper into the chapter. By the way, *believe* in the original is *pisteuó*[13] which actually means to *trust in*.

Finally, while it may become common to *contend with* and *debate over* some of the topic matter presented in this chapter, stating the above distinction early on may prevent some unnecessary disagreements with fellow believers. *(If you're not yet saved you are along for the ride.)* It is my hope by citing these sometimes difficult and somewhat challenging scriptural distinctions, you will experience a new level of grace; perhaps a grace you have yet to come to appreciate and embrace.

The Holy Spirit Leads You to Truth

Theologians much more *schooled* than most of us sheep (unless you are one of those theologians) comment on this issue of *one nature* or *two natures*, quite emphatically. It's nothing new to me and perhaps nothing new to you, to recognize Christian's debating over a number of scripture-based topics. This one appears to be no exception.

However, it may not have been so apparent until now because you will likely find more Christians holding to a *two-natured* view versus a *one-natured* view. Let's make sure we remember, though: holding to what the truth is has never been a popularity contest or a popular thing, for that matter. It would seem reasonable to expect good reasons—representing either nature viewpoint—should be considered and examined. Degrading insults and immediate cries of *"Heresy!"* every time a fellow believer's view differs from one's own is not God's will.

In the Spirit of Christ, I think we need to allow for some latitude when discussing these deep, theological revelations from our Lord. I have spent years extending grace and latitude to a dualistic view evidenced by the simple fact I never questioned it.

However, once I personally began to attribute all of my struggles with some *old* identity fighting against my *new* identity, I sensed within myself division. I had resigned to the idea I would be fighting *myself* until the Lord put me on the other side of this life.

My understanding of the truth—as no longer an advocate for the believer possessing two natures, but rather just one nature—is a *fallible* view of the truth. Let me also remind you those who hold to an alternate, two-nature view *equally* carry a *fallible* understanding of the truth. The Holy Spirit leads us to all truth.

After taking an objective view at both sides, I contemplated my personal experiences in light of scripture. I will finalize things with a prayer request for wisdom. God has demonstrated to me He is happy to reveal Himself, as well as supply wisdom where there is lack. This identity issue is so important. We have to get this right!

"Lord, when I trusted your Word, You changed me and revealed to me my true identity after years of not knowing. You know it was because I hadn't turned the key. This identity matter for my life and for the lives of all of your children could be re-examined because of the release of this book. Therefore, I pray a simple prayer requesting wisdom to better understand what to make over these opposing views within the Body of Christ. Help me to make some sense of it standing upon your Word, and then bless others with it so they'd be who You re-created them to be. Thank You, Father. Thank You, Jesus. Thank You, Holy Spirit!"

I believe the Holy Spirit has compelled me to write this book. The Lord knows exactly where I am in writing this book. My desire is to know my true identity by His sacrifice and revelation—enough to walk as the true new creation He created and intended. It is also to offer encouragement and exhortation to you!

Encouraged and comforted, I sense God telling me to *not shrink back*! Pushing forward you will be challenged with a *key highlight* of the Gospel of grace; your true identity. I give God all of the glory for what He is doing!

Within the Body of Christ, the debate over whether a believer has one nature or two natures appears to experience congestion when getting into the area of sin, or committing sin. A big question, if not the biggest question, is: *"Why then, do those with the 'new birth', the 'new creations' still sin? Why does a believer who is re-created with a divine nature fall short of God's will at certain times?"*

I have observed some who reject the notion the believer can be one-natured, appear to represent a position one *must have* a sinful nature to commit sin. May I interject something to consider on the above reasoning? It is this:

While this following analogy isn't completely *apples-to-apples* on all levels, it can be taken into account when questioning why a new creation is capable of sinning. Here's a basic question:

"Did Adam and Eve require a sin nature to sin against God, in the Garden of Eden?"

The answer to this appears to be, *"No."* They did not originally carry a sinful nature because they had a divine nature. God made everything and it was, *"very good."* Adam and Eve did not inherit a sinful nature because they were unblemished, without sin. They had spiritual life. They did not *come to be* post-fall, as we did, isn't that right? We may not, as believers, come into full agreement as to why Adam and Eve ended up committing sin while simultaneously *not* possessing a *sinful nature*, or an *old self.*

Regardless, Christians like everybody else since Adam and Eve did in fact inherit the cancer of sin. It was passed along through Adam as a result of the fall, according to the Bible. We can likely *also* agree they made a *choice* to disobey God on the matter of the forbidden fruit. Wouldn't you agree?

Even so, as *One New Dude*, you are not in this same, hopeless predicament. You may carry the cancer of sin in your body, but this isn't intended by God to determine your identity. Nor is it to lock you into being *divided as a person* within your unredeemed body.

This is why Jesus came! Jesus came so those who were *degenerate (i.e. every single human being on the planet)* would—by divine intervention—be offered a gift which would *re-generate* them: The Holy Spirit! Praise the Risen King! He is the same Holy Spirit who will guide you into all truth.

Varying Nature Viewpoints

The believer's nature strikes me as quite an important matter as it's being discussed within the Body of Christ. This personal opinion is formed based upon my own life's experience. I have yet to notice anything approaching its magnitude and implications. *"Who am I? Who am I, now that I have accepted Christ into my life? Who has God re-created me to be? Do I have two natures, or just one? When all of my flesh, tendons, ligaments and bones are stripped away, who am I?"*

God spoke everything into being by His Word. Yet, can He not supernaturally take away the redeemed person's *sin nature*, forever... starting with the Cross and *stepped into* at the moment of conversion? Why wouldn't He be able to do so, based upon the finished work at Calvary—especially when *He has spoken and told us He has?*

Based upon my own experience I have drawn a troubling conclusion. Many more followers of Jesus appear to *disagree* with a one-natured view, than agree with it. This *does not* need to remain to be the case. Also, I'd like to share an analogy regarding this, if I may?

Let's say you informed a non-Christian Jesus is coming back anytime soon now because the Bible tells you so. Then, you might also inform them they have to *lose their life to save it*, according to Jesus. No sooner are you done speaking they look at you and shake their head in disgust.

"Huh? I think you're nuts!" Next, they get very angry and then tell you they strongly disagree with you. After some huffs and puffs, they offer up a few reasons to try to justify their disagreement with you. They then turn around and walk away.

May I ask you this? Based upon what they *said* or how they reacted, did this at all change the related text within the Bible? Did their disagreement cause Jesus to decide to change his mind, then miraculously edit and re-write all of the scriptures to which this person did not agree?

Of course it didn't and of course He didn't. God's Word stood. There could have been dozens of discussions which would normally ensue surrounding those scripture references. Yet, what the Holy Spirit said stood. God's Word stood solid and firm. *Unshaken!* Isn't that right?

In the same sense, I would invite you to allow God to reveal truth to you. To *continue* to reveal truth *to* and *through* you, that is. God is so patient! He wants you to know who you are, in Jesus! If it takes you 9 or 999 times to read and believe what God is saying, so let it be! God is patient and God is good!

Recently, I heard an internationally known and televised Pastor/Teacher had a change of mind when it came to believing he had two natures, a sinful nature and a divine nature. Apparently, after some years, he no longer believes such a thing is true.

Have you ever come across a Bible teacher/Pastor who is humble enough to admit they've changed their mind with regard to a specific Bible verse or passage? Isn't it refreshing? I've seen and heard about it on more than one occasion and my respect for them grew immediately.

If respected Bible expositors can *hold passionately to* and *argue persuasively from* a well-researched doctrinal position, then one day see it in a new way—is it possible for any of us to reconsider our current view, as well? Can we too find the same comfort and benefit in changing our mind as we stand upon God's holy and eternal word? Might I suggest you can? If you belong to Jesus then nobody can snatch you from your Father's hand.

"Ask and it will be given to you; seek and you will find; knock and the door will be opened to you."
~ **Matthew 7:7 NIV**

My sincere desire is to encourage people all over the world and specifically *you*, to take a closer look at what God is saying regarding who you really are, in Christ. *He's been saying it for around a few thousand years!*

Permit me to also suggest you not be intimidated by other believers who teach or advocate a different view than what is presented in this book. Many may disagree, but the Holy Spirit in me and my renewed mind is neither calling them names nor accusing them of being false teachers.

In the same way, you and I can have a different viewpoint while not automatically be accused of heresy or being unkind. No matter what view you end up holding to, you will always find other very well-respected, educated and spirit-filled Christians who see things in a different way.

The challenge for you—and it's a very worthwhile challenge—is to decide if you're going to go *all the way* with grace. Will you trust fully in what God says about you as *One New Dude*...or not? God's desire is for you to accept *all* of the grace He is offering. Varying viewpoints regarding how many natures you have as a Christ-follower highly suggests that in the end, only one view can be correct.

Are you willing to take a step out of your comfort zone? Let's go! The Holy Spirit, as always, sets the bar. God is interested in building your faith and revealing even more truth to you. Will you discover your true identity on this journey? It's time. Let's keep moving!

Turning the Key

Since this coming verse is what appears to have been used by God to stop me in my tracks, perhaps it is also the verse which will cause you to stop in your tracks, as well. Let's define, *"turning the key"* as the combination of both *receiving and believing*, OK?

Additionally, this verse is similar to the rest of God's Word: it must be taken in faith. It's not to be glossed over and easily dismissed. We must make sure we are accepting what God is saying with a child-like faith. Else… truth may never be fully realized in our life and in our being. Does this sound fair enough?

Faith requires *activation*.[14] For me, activation was *not* accomplished by setting up a bunch of arguments against what God was saying in favor of what *I* thought was right or correct. God instructs us to lean not on our own understanding, but rather to trust Him, right? When I simply trusted what He had stated in His Word, my whole perspective changed regarding my actual identity. This was my issue! Maybe it's yours? It required of me to let go of old thinking. What was demanded of me, if I were to remain in good conscience, was to embrace a biblically accurate and biblically consistent position when it came to my true nature.

It was not until my faith was *activated* that my whole perspective changed when it came to my identity. Something was different. I felt this huge weight off of my shoulders! Perhaps it was because I had been psychologically carrying around a *sin nature* that no longer needed to be carried around? It forced me to find some other answer, some other *location*, to account for my sin. If I could reconcile this aspect, I'd be more able to accept I *was* really new. I mean—I *knew* I *was new*—but this was going to be a whole *new newness!*

The more I resolved God was telling me something—but I hadn't been trusting Him on it—I encountered a new perspective on life; a *new outlook*. It was one I had never encountered before. It was *fresh*. It wasn't condemning at all. *It was liberating!* You can have it today, just as easily.

Let it be stated: a *jacked-up* theology wasn't required in order to hold to a belief I no longer possessed a sinful nature. I'm just reading my Bible. *Nor was I claiming to be without sin!* Some may try to accuse you of claiming to be without sin, if you adopt this scripturally-sound position of no longer having a sin nature. This would be—as far as I can see—falling short of God's best. Making hasty and inaccurate judgments is not God's best for his children. Visit John 7:24.

Sometimes, as forgiven sinners we over-complicate things. God says something clearly, but we're not fully persuaded. So, we make long lists of why God must mean something other than what He's stated.

We struggle with faith. Maybe we haven't allowed God to sprinkle our hearts with Christ's blood that we would no longer suffer from a guilty conscience? God has made provision through Jesus. Apply his blood and receive what *He has done*. Christ's grace floods your life!

If those around you prefer to hang onto this idea of a *sin nature or old man* duking it out with the new man, you will have to decide in faith what the best way to proceed is. My personal suggestion is no matter what direction you take or decisions you make, always remember to honor Christ with your conduct. You *need not respond in kind* if you are insulted or mocked for living up to what God has already given to you.

God is offering you an opportunity to take comfort that a new life, one without a sin nature, is yours for the receiving. Dude, you are *One New Dude* supernaturally re-created by Jesus, your Savior. *God's not even kidding about it!*

This key is waiting to be *turned*. Have you *turned the key*, yet? God calls you to believe & receive just as He does with any person of faith.

In your case, as was the same in my case, you will need to *"turn the key"* on these identity verses by settling each of them in your mind and heart. It is my conviction that—until this matter of the *flesh having already been crucified to those who belong to Jesus* is trusted as truth—you will not have realized all of what God has for you. Either you *are dead* and *He lives*, or the old you is *still alive*.

Is it not reasonable to conclude—and I say this with brotherly love—there is no belief or trust demonstrated when God is not taken at his Word? Yet, all you need to do is *turn the key! It's that simple!* God is patiently waiting. If you have to change your mind, and I would suggest this is central, change your mind. Just as every breath is an opportunity for the unsaved to trust Christ with their life for salvation, so is every breath an opportunity for the Christian to trust Christ for *complete, pure grace and sanctification*.

As a loving parent holds open their arms to their child who stands apprehensively on the side of the swimming pool, so has God called you into His rest. It's in trusting what God says about your identity where you will be renewed in your mind and walk as *One New Dude!*

Absorbing Truth

Now, start also receiving these other verses to undergird you in your *newfound newness! It's newfound newness* because if you have never taken the above verse as true and a *done deal* within your heart, how could it ever be a settled matter? The same applies to the following *verses below*. Of what profit is it to you for God's truth be revealed to you but never accepted as true and a done deal? Where's the faith there? Oh, to be saved by grace *through faith* and yet so many people shrug off the faith portion. Any dead fish floating down the stream can do that. This isn't you, *One New Dude!*

As Christians, we are to use our gifts to build each other up, isn't this right? Others may want to have their cake and eat it to, but I'm exhorting you—on the authority of God's Word—to *let go of the old* that you may embrace the *new*. Stop giving the *old dude* any thought! *He's crucified at the cross of Christ* and it's all over for him!

The very moment a thought or inclination enters into your mind that is contrary to your divine nature—you make the decision where the thought goes. Thoughts *grow up*, too. If you don't take this thought captive to the obedience of Christ and deal with it properly, you can easily find yourself in condemnation. Since you live in an unredeemed body with a scarred soul that is undergoing construction, the first thing attacked is your identity. *"I couldn't possibly be a new creation."*

Be encouraged. Your Heavenly Father's desire for you is to be *unshakable* on the identity matter!

When you know who you are in Christ, you can immediately take any thought captive to the obedience of Christ. You take up your sword and speak truth to yourself and others. You are a child of God! *One New Dude!* Sin isn't your master, Jesus is! Sin doesn't reign, you reign—thru Jesus!

The enemy wants you to make a big deal out of the fact the cancer of sin still resides in your soon-to-be-redeemed body. What he doesn't want you to do is claim your true identity; your *sonship!* He doesn't want you intentionally stomping on lies and hell all around you while trusting God for how He sees you now.

The enemy prefers much more you'd walk around with a false humility; busy telling everybody how much of a sinner you are instead of how much Jesus did to make you a saint! This isn't the power of positive thinking I'm sharing with you, either. This is God speaking truth into your life! You are responsible to take what is revealed and trust what God says. *Dude up!*

You either have an old man who is *still alive* in you or an *old man/sin nature* who is *dead.* It can't be both—at the same time—in the same sense. Getting this one wrong impacts your daily life, at a minimum. How will you interact with others, how will you think about God, and what is your view of grace? The impact of how these questions are answered hinge upon who you believe you truly are.

We can and will specify a place of allocation for the possibility you may sin, on occasion. Hopefully, this will encourage you to redirect your focus from *sin* to *righteousness.* God has recreated, revealing eternal truth to you that you *may not sin.* It's not *when* you sin, it's *if* you sin. That's good news!

You don't have to claim to be *without sin* to lead a life that is *blameless* and *not mastered by sin*—like it used to be! God doesn't want you focusing on sin. You are dead to it. Focus on Jesus and your Father's great love for you, instead. Branches don't struggle to bear fruit. They merely *abide* in the vine and the vine bears fruit through them. Abide in Jesus by focusing upon Him; not sin and the Law. *"Do this, don't do that!"* The Law's main purpose has always been as a tutor to lead people to faith in Jesus. He's the One who will bear fruit in your life!

First things first, though. God wants you to experience his goodness today in a new, refreshing and exciting way! God speaks to you when you are ready to hear him, I have found. If God keeps taking you through certain passages in the Bible, I would propose God is trying to show you something. He uses other people to communicate with us. It's exactly what He did to me, and still does to me. It's through others & his Word, by his Spirit. Let's check out some other verses, briefly. They might offer additional encouragement to you in grabbing hold of your new identity in Jesus. *Ready? C'mon…let's keep goin'!*

Sinking Your Roots

After *turning the key* on Galatians 5:24, my outlook began to change. God started showing to me the things I needed to know as I pressed in deeper to who He was telling me I now was. This added a whole new level to *not putting new wine into old wineskins*, to be sure!

What God was telling me is what God is now telling you. *Father, fill the reader's mind and heart with the wonderful conviction of what You have done and reveal to them who they now are, in Christ's mighty name, amen!*

Colossians 2: 11-12 NLT
11When you came to Christ, you were "circumcised," but not by a physical procedure. Christ performed a spiritual circumcision—the <u>cutting away of your sinful nature</u>. 12For <u>you were buried with Christ</u> when you were baptized. And with him you were raised to new life because you trusted the mighty power of God, who raised Christ from the dead.

Q. Any indications of a living or active *old you* or *sinful nature?*

This isn't about your efforts, Dude! It's about what *your King has done! Hallelujah!* When you truly *receive* is when you will *reign in life, through Him!* All you have to do is trust what God says!

This key is waiting to be *turned*.

Father, thank You for this Reader. Lord, You sent Your only Son for them!

They are precious in Your sight, Lord. You have demonstrated this and made it widely known! At this moment, I bind this power of confusion which might be in their lives—regarding who they are, in Christ. Let them grab hold of these scriptures and I pray You sink them into the deepest, most inner nooks and crannies of their soul. You are the mighty Savior, Creator and Re-Creator, Father. In Christ's Supreme & Mighty Name, amen!

Colossians 2: 13,14

"You were dead because of your sins and because <u>your sinful nature was not yet cut away</u>. <u>Then God made you alive with Christ</u>, for he forgave all our sins. He canceled the record of the charges against us and took it away by nailing it to the cross."

Q. Any indications of a living or active *old you* or *sinful nature?*

This key is just waiting to be turned, isn't it? Turn that thing!

"TURNING THE KEY"

God Speaks:

"And those who belong to Christ Jesus have crucified the flesh with its passions and desires."
~Galatians 5:24 ESV

TRUST WHAT GOD SAYS

"YOU WERE DEAD BECAUSE OF YOUR SINS AND BECAUSE YOUR SINFUL NATURE WAS NOT YET CUT AWAY. THEN GOD MADE YOU ALIVE WITH CHRIST, FOR HE FORGAVE ALL OUR SINS. HE CANCELED THE RECORD OF THE CHARGES AGAINST US AND TOOK IT AWAY BY NAILING IT TO THE CROSS." ~ COLOSSIANS 2:13,14 NLT

"FOR YOU HAVE DIED"
"NO LONGER I WHO"

"THOSE WHO BELONG TO CHRIST JESUS HAVE CRUCIFIED THE SINFUL NATURE WITH ITS PASSIONS AND DESIRES."
~GALATIANS 5:24 NIV

Turning the Key Finds True Rest

"Let us therefore strive to enter that rest, so that no one may fall by the same sort of disobedience."
~ **Hebrews 4:11 ESV**

Full rest is important to God. Jesus Christ passed the test you and I never could or would pass. He lived a perfect, sinless life! He's done all that needed to be done in order to bring you into an everlasting relationship with your Heavenly Father. This is for certain.

Now, all you have to do is to *receive. Grace is a gift!* This matter of what Christ did for you with respect to your sinful nature at the Cross, exponentially ramps up and takes to a whole new level the *grace stakes*. What are *grace stakes?* They are not anything you throw on the grill —I can tell you that! We're talking about them throughout this book. *Amazing grace, how sweet the sound!*

If we don't receive *all of grace,* then we are by default rejecting it. None of us desire to be on this side, do we? Heck no! I certainly don't! Do you remember the Judaizers in the Book of Galatians? They were trying to *add* to what Jesus had already accomplished on the cross—the free gift of salvation.

What did they do? It was, *"Jesus plus..."* remember? The Judaizers were attempting to enforce the idea one must be physically circumcised in order to be a Christian. By doing so, whether they meant to or not, they were conveying what Jesus did was not enough. Rather, you needed to add to his work by way of physical circumcision serving as the additional requirement.

The general idea of the above analogy is: if anybody adds to what Jesus has done then it's not grace. If Jesus dealt with the sin nature at the cross but a person is attempting to accomplish a portion of his finished work on their own, it's the same as trying to kill an old self who is already dead— is it not? Christ's sacrifice cut away your *sin nature*—your *old self*—your *old man*. If in turn you don't acknowledge *and* accept this finished work—aren't your *crucifixion* efforts *adding* to what Christ has accomplished? Doesn't this then become an issue of accepting or rejecting God's grace? Choosing to achieve what's already been achieved is not really *receiving*, is it?

If this is you, this isn't intended to be a guilt trip. Before God turned up the dial on this one, my thinking was just as I described above. Most of my Christian life I had never turned the key on the crucial verses which are in this book. I now have and continue to do so as Jesus sprinkles my heart with his blood and converts my soul, washing me clean with his Word. Only God's truth *believed and received* will ever bring a person into the fullness of God's grace. Is it not a worthwhile pursuit? Diligently seek God on this identity matter— even when you are certain you already have. To do so will set you up for tremendous blessing!

Getting back to the initial point, there is an analogy the Lord gave to me I'd like to share. Maybe it will give you even more to lock onto when you are considering what Jesus did for you in order to make you *One New Dude*. It is regarding this Judaizer's *addition* attempt at Christ's finished work, which involves the *requirement of* or *addition of* a *physical* circumcision.

Ironically, what happened back in Galatia parallels this matter of *two natures* versus *one nature* in a certain sense. This idea came as a surprise to me, because it wasn't initially on my radar. It's an interesting analogy, though. Let's take quick look at it.

When a person forces the explanation of any believer's sin into a *bucket* or *bucket item* labeled, *"sinful nature,"* then this *adds to* what reasonably appears to have already been *cut away*. There was a *spiritual circumcision* performed and accomplished by God himself, in Christ. A *finished work* as far as the *sinful nature*, the *old self*, the *old man* goes. While it does cleanse once for all time all sin of the *One New Dude*, it doesn't *remove* the cancer of sin. There's still indwelling sin in a believer's *members*, according to God, through Paul.

Even so, Christ's finished work *does* break sin's power in the *One New Dude*. It *does forgive* all sin, and it *does replace* the old man. Christ's blood is constantly cleansing the believer. The Judaizer's reasoning mixes old and new covenants. Isn't it interesting what they were attempting to add in the *physical*, Christ had included in the *spiritual*? Christ circumcised the *One New Dude's* heart! *That's hardcore!* You have already stepped into this as a Christian. Now, you've got to *turn the key* on what God has told you. *You can do this!*

What Jesus did for you and me is a gift. We must accept it or by default, push it away. You didn't push grace away when Jesus saved you, so why would you want to push away the substance of this grace, which directly deals with who He has re-created you to be? This includes the drastic measures He went to in order to free you from your *old self!*

I understand. This can take a little to wrap our minds around, but so can walking on water or breathing galaxies into existence!

Nevertheless, you and I must accept what God has done and what God has revealed. This is why we are saved by grace, *through faith*. Amen? It's a gift *(grace)* which requires trust *(faith.)* God gives even more grace and God understands where you are with the whole thing, too. God is for you! He sent his only Son for you, so you *know* He's on your team! If God is for you, who can be against you?

Praise the living King! He has done it all! God is a giver! Christ ministers. Christ serves. Christ saves. Christ cuts away the old. Christ creates new creatures in Him! *Hallelujah!* What a Savior! *Rejoice!* Your King will complete the work He began within you!

Ask, seek, knock. Jesus said, "It is finished."

Romans 6:4 NASB
"We were buried therefore with him by baptism into death, in order that, just as Christ was raised from the dead by the glory of the Father, we too might walk in newness of life."

Q. Any indications of a living or active *old you* or *sinful nature?*

"TURNING THE KEY"

God Speaks:

"And those who belong to Christ Jesus have crucified the flesh with its passions and desires."
~Galatians 5:24 ESV

TRUST WHAT GOD SAYS

"WE WERE BURIED THEREFORE WITH HIM BY BAPTISM INTO DEATH, IN ORDER THAT, JUST AS CHRIST WAS RAISED FROM THE DEAD BY THE GLORY OF THE FATHER, WE TOO MIGHT WALK IN NEWNESS OF LIFE."
~ROMANS 6:4 NASB

"FOR YOU HAVE DIED"
"NO LONGER I WHO"

"THOSE WHO BELONG TO CHRIST JESUS HAVE CRUCIFIED THE SINFUL NATURE WITH ITS PASSIONS AND DESIRES."
~GALATIANS 5:24 NIV

**Ask. Seek. Knock.
Jesus said, "It is finished."**

Romans 6:6 ISV
"<u>We know that our old natures were crucified with him</u> so that our sin-laden bodies might be rendered powerless and we might no longer be slaves to sin."

Q. Any indications of a living or active *old you* or *sinful nature*?

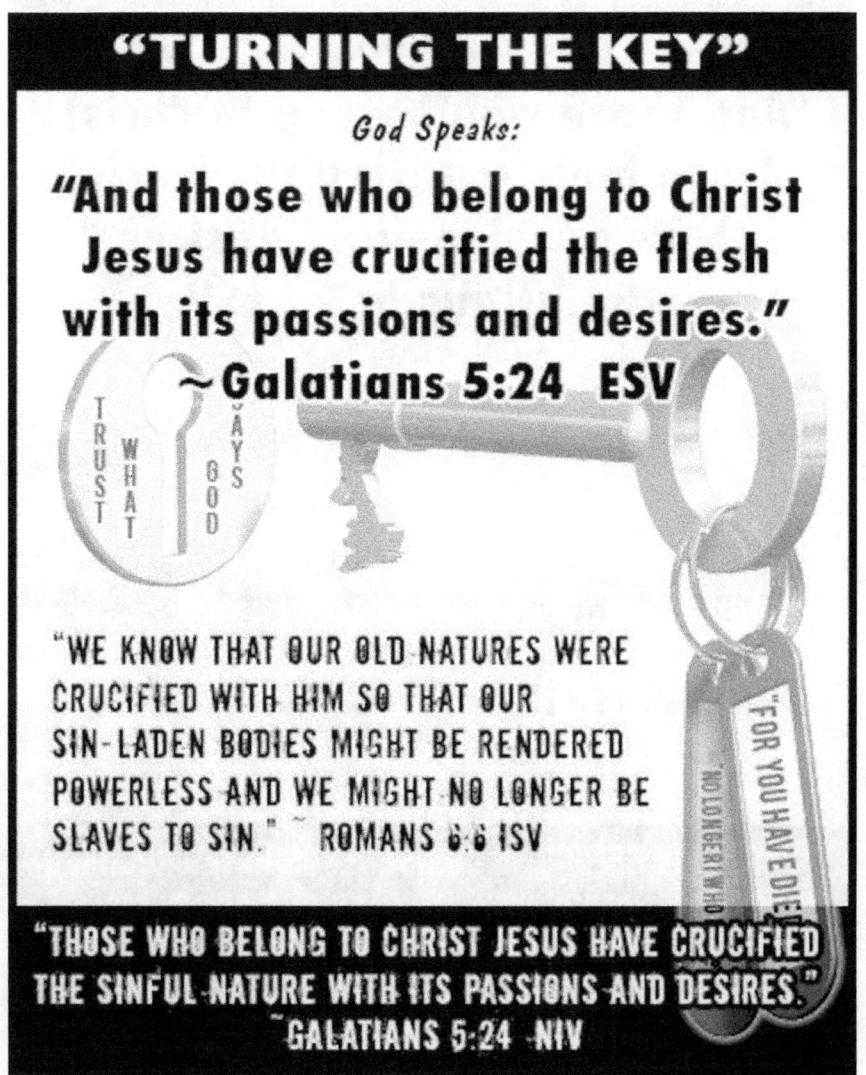

Romans 6:8 NLT
"And <u>since we died</u> with Christ, we know we will also live with him."

Q. Any indications of a living or active *old you* or *sinful nature?*

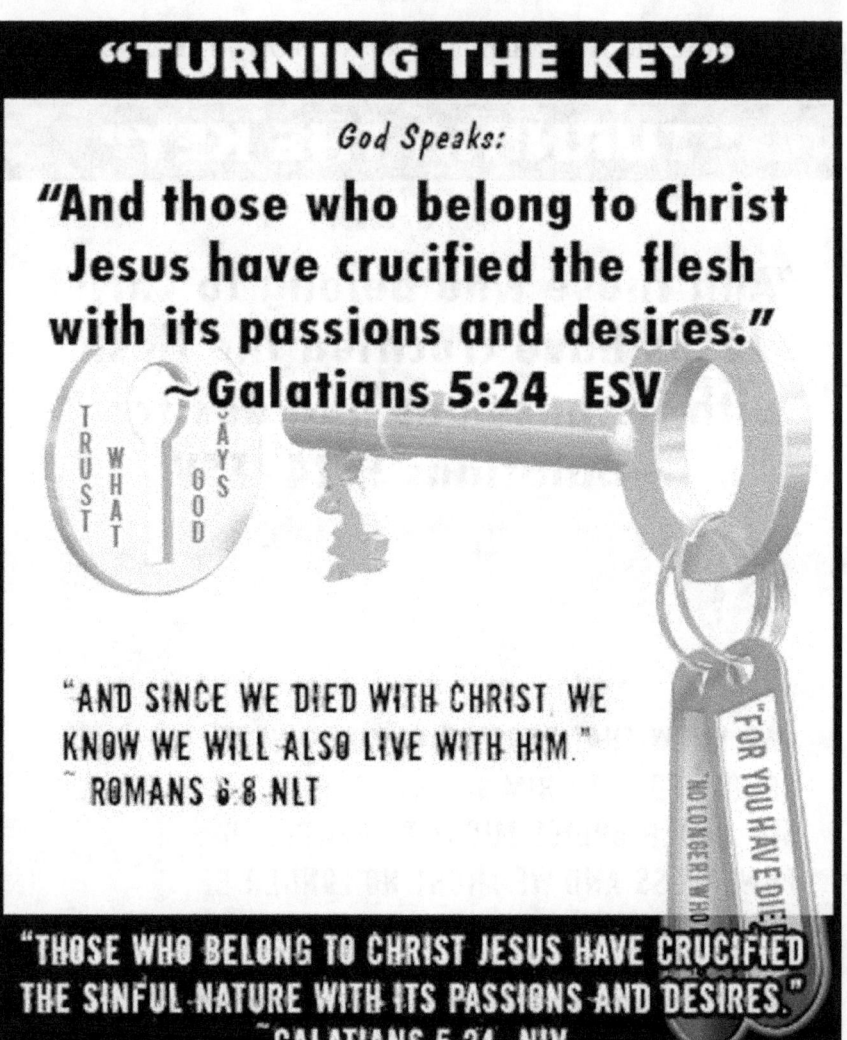

Paul Turned the Key

Not only is it Paul who God is using to tell us all about the sinful nature being crucified already, but God uses Paul to also show us what it is to accept grace.

You see, it's obvious Paul knew his sinful nature had already been crucified. Paul knew he was a recipient of grace. Expressing he wasn't worthy of any of God's grace—called to be an apostle—gave a strong indication he felt a great sense of *unworthiness*.

Yet, Paul still accepted what Christ did for him at the cross. He still embraced he was a new creature and his old self *was no more*. He embraced and taught Christ's work was complete. He taught once and for all time—by Christ's finished work and his own election as a Christian —his old, sinful nature was no longer. This applies to all Christ-followers. Will you receive it completely, just as Paul did?

"Father of Faith" Turned the Key

Abraham, often referred to as the *"Father of Faith,"* was faced with multiple calls from God to *turn the key*. God had brought Abraham (then Abram), out of Ur of the Chaldeans. Abraham had indeed *turned the key* when he left Haran to go to a land God would show him. He believed God would show him the land and he also received the gift and promise of the land, which was Canaan.

Another time Abraham had to *turn the key* was when this test came:

Here, we have a situation where God had promised to make Abraham the father of a multitude of nations. This is what God declared to him:

> *"...for I have made you the father of a multitude of nations."*
> **Genesis 17:5 ESV**

Did you catch that? God *had already made* Abraham something he still had to embrace. Abraham could have said, *"I disagree, God. That doesn't sound like me. My thinking doesn't match up with this and I don't quite get it all. So, no... I'm not whatever it is you are telling me. That's crazy, God."* Abraham chose not to do this.

God was *telling Abraham* what was up! God wasn't asking Abraham for his opinion, right? God was basically laying it down. *"Dude, here's what <u>I have made you</u>: the father of a multitude of nations. This is who you are. I've said it, it's on. Now, what is your response?"*

In one sense, it was still unfolding. The descendants were forthcoming. This would take time. In another sense and simultaneously, it was a done deal! As Abraham stood there, that's exactly who he was. He was what God said he was. He was the father of a multitude of nations. God said it and it was up to Abraham to believe and receive it. Abraham had to *turn the key!*

Could Abraham explain it all? Let's agree: no he couldn't explain it all. His sight could not and your sight cannot see past the present. Did it make it any less true he couldn't explain it all? Let's agree, again: no it didn't. Was what was to come next going to make his life easier? Probably not, but let's drop in on God's next set of instructions and testing for him:

"Take now your son, your only son, whom you love, Isaac, and go to the land of Moriah, and offer him there as a burnt offering on one of the mountains of which I will tell you."
~ Genesis 22:2 NASB

"Huh?" Is it possible this phrase may have been on your mind or my mind; were we in his very place? Especially, if we remind ourselves of Isaac's significance as it relates to Abraham being *"the father of a multitude of nations?"* Isaac was *supposed to be* and *promised to be* part of this plan:

"...for through Isaac shall your offspring be named."
~ Genesis 21:12 ESV

Did Abraham say, *"I know you've shown me You are trustworthy, God. However, I don't really get where you are going with this. How's this going to work though, God? I'm not moving until you explain it all."*

Dude, you didn't fail in faith when you trusted Christ as your

Savior, did you? So, you prove by your own experience *one must not fail* in faith. You aren't *doomed* to consistently fail in faith. That's not very encouraging and not very *new covenant!*

Therefore, while you are to participate in the putting to death the *deeds* of your old nature by the Spirit of God, you by no means are to put to death what is already revealed to be dead. This would be adding to Christ's finished work, as previously mentioned. When a gift is offered true humility believes and receives what God is offering.

"So the promise is received by faith. It is given as a free gift. And we are all certain to receive it, whether or not we live according to the Law of Moses, if we have faith like Abraham's. For Abraham is the father of all who believe."
~ Romans 4:16 NLT

While this previous verse is used in perhaps a different context, it would still follow the promise of God is to be received by faith. When it comes to what Christ has accomplished at the cross on your behalf, God calls you to receive it by faith. You may not understand how it was all achieved but this does not mean it did not occur. *Worship your King! You are more than a conqueror because of what He did and the key you turn!*

Esther & Mary Turned the Key

Esther. Have you considered Esther and Mary? Both of these great women of God *turned the key*.

If you recall, had it not been for Esther's intervention, the Israelite people would have been annihilated. Jesus Messiah was prophesied to appear from the Davidic lineage. With Haman at the helm of this satanic plot to wipe out the Jewish people, the Messiah's Davidic lineage would be interrupted and crumble. Not a small situation! How then will men's crimes have opportunity to be pardoned before a holy God? Men need a Savior and his name is the name above every name, Jesus!

But God... aren't those great words? But God orchestrated

the situation for Mordechai to make an appeal to his niece, Esther:

> *"Don't think for a moment that because you're in the palace you will escape*
> *when all other Jews are killed. If you keep quiet at a time like this, deliverance and relief for the Jews will arise from some other place, but you and your relatives will die. Who knows if perhaps you were made queen for just such a time as this?"*
> **~ Esther 4:13-14 NLT**

Recognizing through a series of events her people were in trouble, Esther realized her time had come. Esther *believed* God had chosen her to stand in the gap of this situation. Esther also *received* the benefits which would ensue, as a result. Esther *turned the key*.

    Mary. What about Mary, the mother of Jesus? Mary turned the key, didn't she?

    One day out of nowhere, God sends the angel Gabriel to bless Mary *enormously!* The angel basically informs Mary she has found favor with God and she will bear a child, the "Son of God."

    When God tells you the *old is gone* and the *new has come*, sometimes it's hard to grasp right away. Mary knew what it was like as God reveals a mind-blowing fact to her. It's understandable she appears a bit confused:

> *"How will this be," Mary asked the angel, "since I am a virgin?"*
> **~ Luke 1:34**

Upon hearing the angel out, it was clear Mary moved from a place of confusion and indecisiveness to a place of single-mindedness and trust. *Mary turned the key.*

> *"I am the Lord's servant," Mary answered. "May it be to me as you have said." Then the angel left her.*
> **~ Luke 1:38**

Galatians 2:20 NLT

"My <u>old self has been crucified</u> with Christ. <u>It is no longer I who live</u>, but Christ lives in me. So I live in this <u>earthly body</u> by trusting in the Son of God, who loved me and gave himself for me."

Q. Any indications of a living or active *old you* or *sinful nature?*

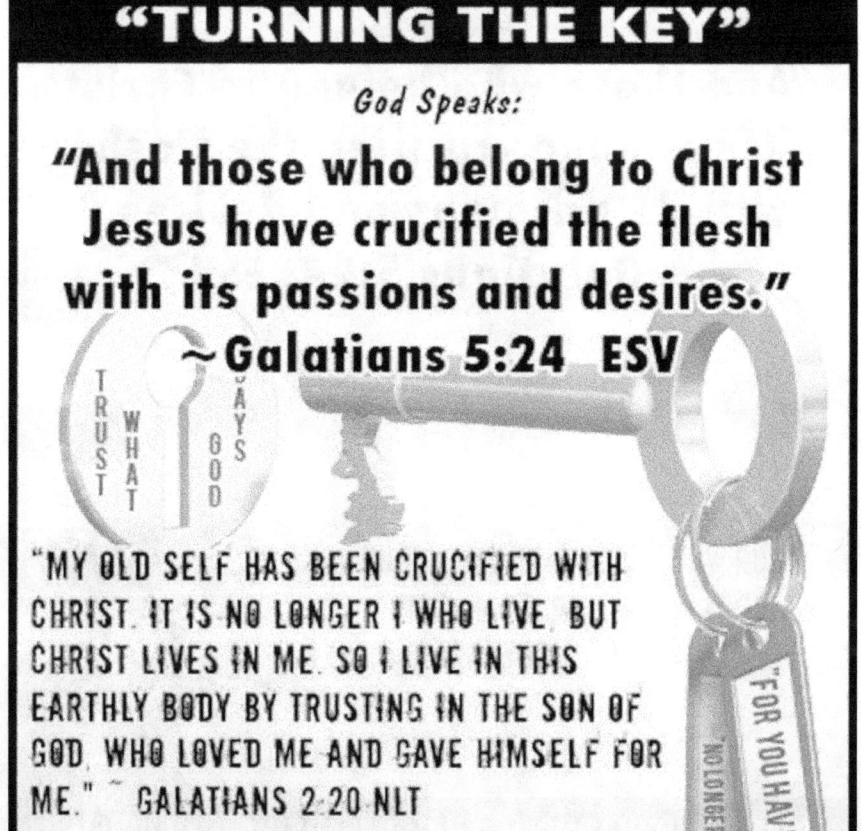

Colossians 3:3 NASB
"For you have died and your life is hidden with Christ in God."

Q. Any indications of a living or active *old you* or *sinful nature?*

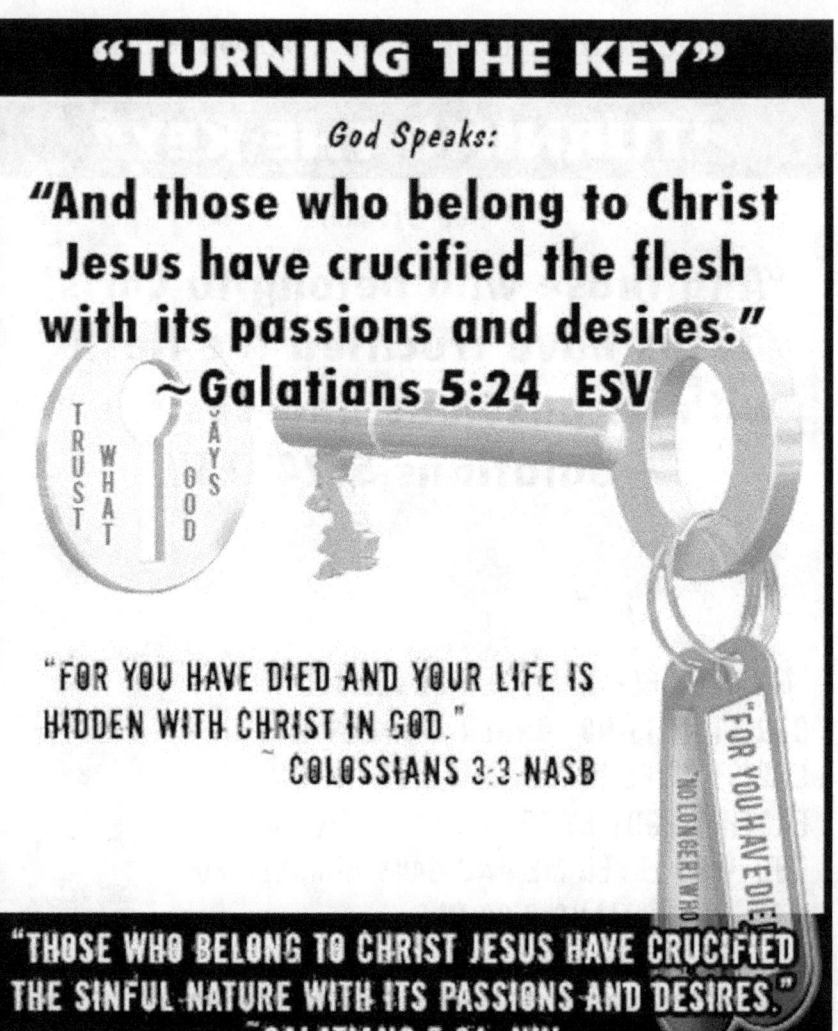

De-Terminator

You may find it helpful to simplify and establish just *what it is* that determines *who you actually are*, when it comes to your true identity. As long as you can rest upon a solid foundation built upon fact, you will be able to weather the storms of life. Since it is Christ's finished work at the Cross and bodily resurrection that establishes your identity, you need only to *turn the key*. Trust what God says. Jesus is God. Scripture is God-breathed. Jesus knew why He was going to the Cross. One major reason, as revealed in Scripture, is He was on a mission to crucify your sinful nature. He accomplished this and wants you to trust scripture.

> *"Therefore everyone who hears these words of Mine and acts on them, may be compared to a wise man who built his house on the rock."*
> **~ Matthew 7:24 NASB**

Let's keep exploring by going back to the beginning, just for a brief few moments. Be sure to take notice of how God establishes your identity. Your identity has always been a gift from God. You can't earn it. You either are a child of God, or you are not.

As *One New Dude*, you certainly are a child of God! Get excited because there's a lot to get excited about as a child of God! The Lord has made you new so you would have a sobering realization of his tremendous grace. Intentionally establish and remind yourself—from this point forward and with every fiber of your being—your identity depends upon God's Spirit.

Get ready for some mind-blowing truths! Get ready to stand for who you really are, all because of Christ. After you see how God establishes your identity, you are going to have to choose how you will *now* identify yourself. Will you carry a false humility, consistently identifying yourself as a sinner? Or, will you carry a true humility, one that accepts complete grace and consistently identifies with others as a *son*?

If you have a habit of dismissing who God says you are because of your past or due to accepting the lies of the enemy, rather than accepting the solid truth of God, change your mind! As Jesus draws lines and demands for people to choose sides, so God is making it clear you can only be a slave to one thing, or the other. You must choose, so let's get going!

Spiritual Condition

Have you ever taken a close look into the ramifications of *"The Fall?"* Were you aware of how what occurred in the Garden of Eden relates to you now, as a Christian? Have you considered how this event directly impacts, determines and defines your nature and true identity, today?

My questions are posed so they might lovingly challenge you to seek out, examine and expeditiously *be* the *One New Dude* God has intended for you to be. It's not *One New Dude* who *shares space*. This does not appear to be God's plan, because Holy Spirit fire is a consuming fire! God blasted out the old dude and re-created you to be *One New Dude*. There's not any room in God's plan for both an old and a new you!

On that note, Jesus never promoted or encouraged indecisiveness; did He? No way! Jesus is always about making up your mind, isn't He? Jesus draws lines. Jesus divides truth from error. Jesus draws out commitments and decisions from people who need to make choices, one way or another. Neutrality is not an option!

Some examples. *"Count the cost."*[15] Or, how about, *"He who is not with Me is against Me."*[16] Or yet another, *"Anyone who puts a hand to the plow and then looks back is not fit for the Kingdom of God.'"*[17] Then, when the rich young ruler approached Him, Jesus also gave him a choice—didn't He?

Jesus knew everything about him so He basically said—in my paraphrase—*"Ok, then… you seriously think you've kept all of the Commandments? Go sell everything you own, give the money to the poor, and follow Me."* Decisions! Life altering, eternity-defining decisions when it comes to Jesus!

Inspired by the exhortations and reasoning of Jesus—the Creator of all—will you *turn the key* and become intentional about your singular identity, which stems from understanding and accepting the nature God has assigned and gifted to you? Jesus went to great lengths to insure you would! Maybe it will offer some additional insight if we take a quick look at the original text, for the word, *"nature?"*

Greek to English
physis: nature[18]
Definition: *nature, inherent nature, origin, birth.*

Now, how about following up with a written timeline of events? This should help you to establish where God places you, today. It should also encourage you and re-enforce to you your true identity, which is rooted in your spiritual condition.

First off, when Adam fell, his *divine nature* immediately switched over to a *fallen or sinful nature*. God's Spirit no longer indwelt and communed intimately, with Adam. Communing intimately in a loving relationship was God's original design for man. God instead, withdrew his Holy Spirit. As promised and warned, Adam died both physically and spiritually. After Adam, man was no longer being made in God's image.

> *"When Adam had lived 130 years, he had a son in his own likeness, in his own image; and he named him Seth."*
> **~ Genesis 5:3 NLT**

Notice, Seth was born just like Adam, *"in his very image"*. God hadn't made Adam in an image which excluded God's Spirit. To the contrary, God communed with his creation of man, via his spirit. *The Fall* messed the whole thing up, as you may well know.

So in the record above, Seth is being born in the same, *jacked up* image. It's an image which does not have God's presence in his spirit-man. Horrific! Spiritually dead. This is not good!

Being born spiritually dead has an impact on the soul. This conceded, your soul does not appear to determine your nature or true identity. That's entirely up to God. Just as God calls the shots on the Moral Law as the Moral Law-Giver, so does God determine what exactly designates a human being as his child. We read:

> *"But to all who did receive him, who believed in his name, he gave the right to become children of God,"*
> **~ John 1:12 NLT**

Clearly, it's God who is setting the determining factors when it comes to an individual's identity. God establishes who we are, from the onset. This appears to always be dependent upon one's relationship with Him. He consistently upholds this reality all of the way through, from generation to generation, individual to individual. We observe this reality from *Creation* to *The Fall*—all of the way to the Cross—then onward past the Cross. When God chooses to adopt any person into his family, on whatever terms He chooses, this is certainly his prerogative. He does what He pleases and it pleased Him to crush his Son on your behalf. *That's an amazing God!*

Finalizing the point being made about the effects of *The Fall*, what I think we can surmise is Adam and Eve *had the Holy Spirit* when they were created. They could not physically and spiritually *die* if they first did not have physical and spiritual *life*.

You and I however, were not filled with God's Spirit when we were born. When you were born, you were not in communion with God because you were born spiritually dead (Psalms 51:5). You grew up in a body which was destined to die. This body has the cancer of sin and you also had a nature which had no spiritual life. *Not good news.* The soul, instead of being *excellent*[19] from the presence of the power of God, was *less than* excellent.

By the way, when you come across portions of this book that discuss the soul as well as any portions that refer to *sanctification*, try to keep in mind there are consequences to the soul as a result of *The Fall*. Being degenerate *demanded* you needed to get back into communion with God. You needed to be *regenerated*.

Does this make sense? It really should. You needed *life!* You needed *spiritual life!* That's why there's an answer to the *bad news* mentioned above. The *good news* of Jesus Christ is the answer!

At the center of your possible identity crisis is likely a type of confusion—a stronghold the enemy uses to his advantage. If you examine your thinking and find the wounds of your soul are causing you to panic and question your identity, then cast those arguments down. Take every thought captive to the obedience of Christ, immediately! Sprinkle Christ's sinless and shed blood all over your mind and heart. Be freed from a guilty conscience! Experience healing, in the name of Jesus! Thank You, Father.

Re-Affirming Truth

Re-affirm to yourself your soul's wounds or your soul's imperfections do not determine your identity or nature. You are what God says you are. You are *One New Dude!* You can't hear this enough! *Hallelujah!* God is crazy on fire for you! Is He catching you on fire, yet? Look at the cross! Look at the empty tomb! Look at his promises! Christ indicated *"if you die, yet shall you live!" Say what?* This world has nothing on Jesus! Let not your heart be troubled. Jesus has overcome the world, and He lives in you! He is Lord and the old you *was crucified* with Him at the cross when you trusted Him as Savior. Now, *turn the key*, if you haven't already! God is good!

So, here are two foundational observations which are intended to pour eternal truth into your soul. You currently fall under one of two *conditions*, as it relates to your spirit and nature:

> **Spiritually Dead:** possessing a fallen, sinful nature - only.
> **Spiritually Alive:** possessing a regenerated, divine nature - only.

Notice as a *"Christ-Receiver"* you received Christ's offer of salvation and asked Him to come into your heart and life and to save you. You confessed something akin to: *"Yes, Jesus. I believe you died for my sins. You are my Lord. I believe God raised you from the dead. I trust You. I will follow You."*

God, the Holy Spirit, regenerated you by making you alive in Christ. Where once you were a different person because God was *not* intimately indwelling you with his presence, you are now *One New Dude* because He is now indwelling you with his presence. You invited God in by your free will, so He blessed you with more than we will cover here! It seems like you chose Jesus, but Jesus really chose you!

You used to really have no true identity, because your job or family role is not eternal. Your sinful nature had alienated you from your Creator, leaving you orphaned. Tragic! This is likely why Jesus chose to put this helpful information out to us when man beheld his glory and as He walked this planet:

"Whoever finds his life will lose it, and whoever loses his life for my sake will find it."
~ Matthew 10:39 NIV

Adam's sin caused you to be born in his likeness, as we have seen…not in God's image. God became a Man in Jesus to rescue and redeem you. Check. You likely *get* this, already. What's critical, though, is you *recognize and hold onto* the biblical revelation of why you are now *One New Dude* as a Christ-Follower.

You were dead then God made you alive in Christ. It is the presence or lack of presence of God's Holy Spirit that determines your nature. A *divine nature* is dependent upon *God's presence.* A *sinful nature does not possess* God's presence. If you have God's presence, you have God's nature. You are a partaker of the divine nature. Jesus won this nature back for you! He said you could only come to the Father through Him, remember?

Also, remember the word and definition for *nature,* above? Nature can refer to *origin,* or *birth,* right? Well, think about it. Jesus said one must be *born again,* if they were to see the kingdom of God. He then continued and talked about the *rebirth*. Let's take a quick look, just for the sake of reference:

"That which is born of the flesh is flesh, and that which is born of the Spirit is spirit."
~ John 3:6 ESV

Notice how the word *nature* is directly related to origin and birth? Your nature is tied into who you are now, as a result of what type of birth(s) you have had. You were born of flesh, so you have a body. Even if you make a concession and lump in the *sinful nature* as part of being what Jesus is referring to above when He says *"flesh,"* you still have a major reference here regarding your identity.

As an aside, don't forget John the Baptist was said to have been *filled with the Holy Spirit* in Elizabeth's womb.[20] This is an exception to the rule when it comes to being born of the flesh.[21] At the same time, it is a unique example illustrating how God can sovereignly cause a baby born of a man and woman to *already be* filled with the Holy Spirit.

Getting back to the verse above, one way of breaking down

what Jesus said might be like this: You were born of flesh, so you inherited a dying, sin-cancer-infected body, along with a sinful nature. You were degenerate. Your nature *(identity)* was sinful because God's presence was not united and in communion with your spirit.

One angle I'd invite you to consider regarding this revelation from Jesus is to temporarily adopt two other ways of saying it and decide if it's still true. I'll use my own words:

"If you have been born of the flesh, you are of a sinful nature. If you have been born of the Spirit, you are of the divine nature." OR: *"If you have only been born of the flesh you are the old man. If you have been born of the Spirit, you are One New Dude."*

Finalizing this thought, when you trusted Christ as your Lord and Savior you were born of the Spirit. So, you became spirit. Your nature *changed* from that of the flesh to that of the spirit. You became spiritually alive and your identity changed to a child of God. All of this occurred because you received Christ's Spirit, the Spirit of God. God saved you. Your nature is of the divine nature. You *inherited* the nature of God. *Astonishing!*

Keep in mind also—the body you inherited is *corruptible*. Yet, this body will be replaced by *incorruptible*. God promises this to his children. Your old nature died because this is how God set it all up. *He knows what He's doing!* God re-created you, all before you even knew what was going on. He had to tell you! He tells each of us. God *reveals*. You *trust. That's your job.* You wanted to do some work? There's your work. Believe on Him, whom He has sent! Amen?

Fully be persuaded. Fully be reminded. Jesus did it all. You trust what He tells you. You keep learning what He did for you. This is what God desires, right? This is God's will; your *sanctification.* Wash your mind with the water of his Word. You were old, now you're new. Out with the old, in with the new! Try repeating it: *"No more old, only new. No more old, only new."* Do it in faith. It's good stuff!

"Yeah, but what about…" Cast it down! No, *"but what about!"* God said it. Tell yourself, *"I'm turning the key! Jesus lives in me. I'm dead, He's alive. He gets all the glory! My identity is in Christ, not my old self. He's taking me home, unredeemed physical body and all. A once troubled soul, now a soul being restored and on its way home. End of story on who I am. I'm a son. I was a sinner, a slave to sin. Now, I'm a son, a slave to righteousness. I walk in*

newness, stomping out lies, casting down arguments! This is faith, and by grace through faith am I saved! Moreover, faith comes by hearing, and by hearing the Word of Christ.[22] *This is what I'm hearing: Those who belong to Christ Jesus have crucified the flesh.'*[23]

God's Spirit is invited into your vessel by you. He infuses you with life! His Spirit brings your spirit back from the dead. He's not bringing *sinful natures* back from the dead. He's bringing *spirits* back from the dead. *Hallelujah!*

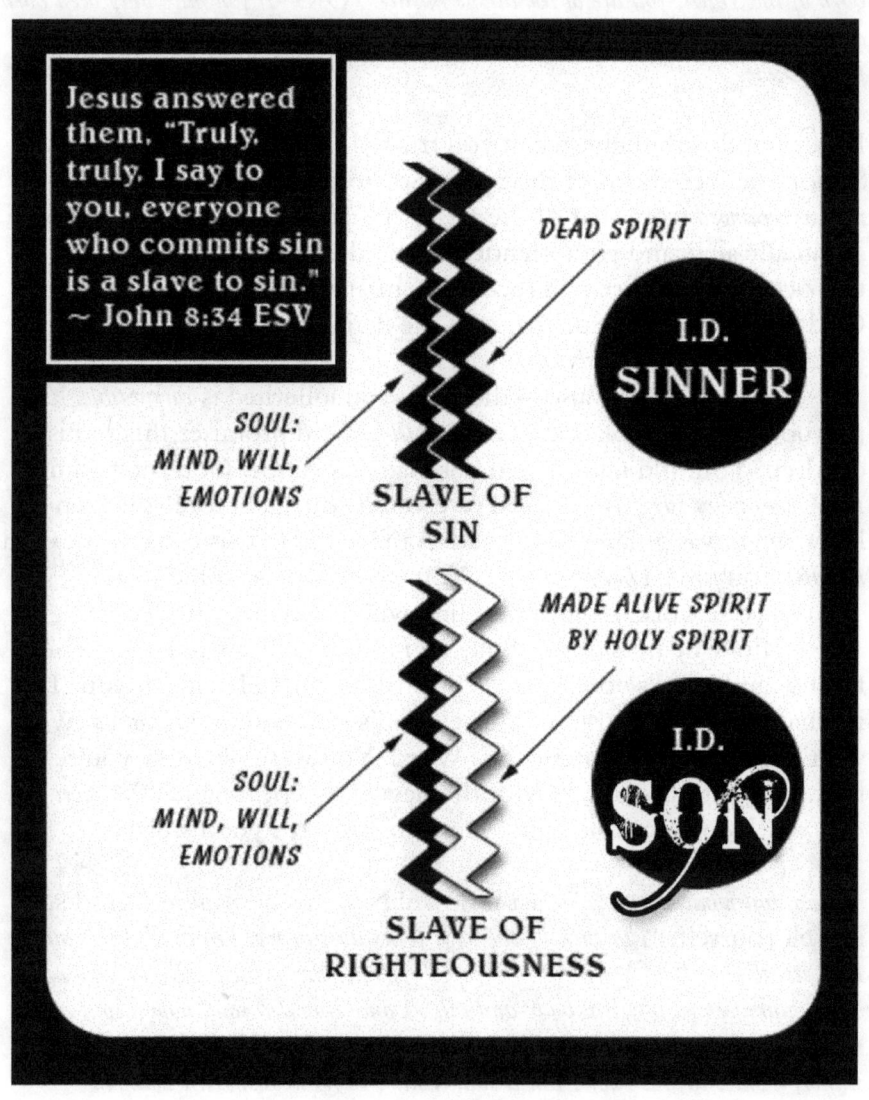

Check Your Charge

The more *take-away's* that encourage you in your true identity, the better. What if we were to look at the simple automobile and pull out a word picture from it? Let's *drive home* this idea of spiritual *condition* determining your nature. Ready? Let's do it.

There are two cars. One has a dead battery; the other has a dead battery, too. However, the second car gets jumped. Who do you think is going to be supplying the power in this analogy? Jesus! That's right!

Look, it's easy. You see it coming. The battery is your spirit. You're the car. You have a body, and the body wraps up and protects the vital components of this car. You have the battery, the wires, the distributor, the engine, the fluids, all of that. Those components comprise and are akin to your soul, let's say.

Every single component doesn't require the battery, as others do. However, if they are going to be part of a car that actually runs, they need the battery just as much! Bottom line is, *enough* important parts of the car depend upon the battery in order for the car to function and do what it was created to do—drive!

So, here you are, represented as the second car. Then, there's an unsaved person who hasn't surrendered to Jesus, as the other car. When you received Jesus as Savior and Lord of your life, Jesus jumped your battery, right? You were a *death-walker* before you received Jesus. You were dead in trespasses and sins. Then, God made you alive, in Christ. *Poof!* Jesus jumped your vessel *(by jumping your spirit)* with his Holy Spirit. Just as the car that got jumped can function and drive, so can you now function and live for God! After all, this is why He created you.

ON JESUS: *"for through him God created everything in the heavenly realms and on earth. He made the things we can see and the things we can't see--such as thrones, kingdoms, rulers, and authorities in the unseen world. Everything was created through him and for him."*
~ Colossians 1:16

Certainly, the other car is still in desperate need of a jump. That whole car has nothing going on. Sure, people drive by and acknowledge it, but what does it matter? It wasn't designed to just sit there and try to look good. It was designed to drive and it isn't fulfilling its purpose! It's a tragedy to anyone who knows the truth about it. All the car needs is a *jump*. Otherwise, it's dead. Seems minor, but it's really everything!

Jesus, on the other hand, is *life* and *good news*. Your *car* got jumped and the vital parts of the car are now reaping the benefits on top of it! Clogged lines and rust will not set in, as *must* be the case of one's spiritually lifeless existence. Those vital parts, indicative of the soul, are now being cleared out, optimized, and are humming! Things are getting shaken up! Oil's getting pumped throughout the engine. By the way, did you know oil is a *type* of the Holy Spirit? The *Ten Virgins*, for example?[24] The Holy Spirit is just what you have and need. He has sealed you for the day of redemption, and Jesus said nobody can take you from the Father's hand.

Does it sound like there's any chance this battery could ever go dead, again? Your *battery* might seem to run low at times. Perhaps you have quenched or grieved the Holy Spirit?

> *"And do not grieve the Holy Spirit of God, with whom you were sealed for the day of redemption."*
> **~ Ephesians 4:30**

Nevertheless and according to the Lord, once He *jumped* your spirit and made you alive in Christ, He sealed you and made you his own for good. God is the *Master Mechanic* of your life and it's all because of Jesus!

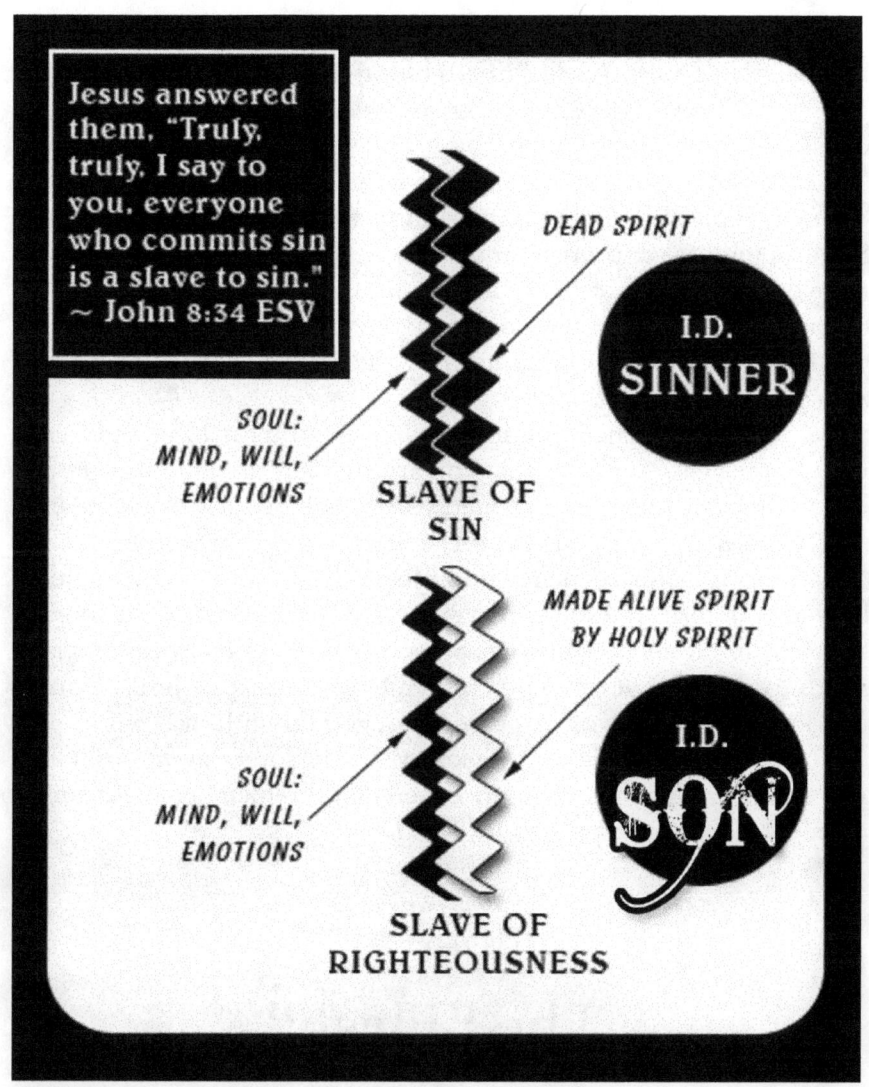

Hopefully, you now *have* or have *further established* within your being just what determines your nature and identity. That *what* is a *Who*, and that *Who* is God. Do not take this matter lightly. You are in the middle of an invisible war. Words matter. Accepting *all* God's grace matters.

    As a son you are a slave to righteousness. You are not a slave to sin. The more you identify with being a sinner, the less you identify with being a son. Being a sinner is old. Being a son is new. All things have become new, in Christ. Don't fall prey to mixing[25] covenants. Don't fall prey to habitually saying you are a sinner, just because it's popular. Once Christ's blood was shed, things changed. The veil was torn. Your heart was sprinkled from a guilty conscience.[26]

New Dudes don't need to know they have sinned. They would have never come to Christ if they didn't see their need for a Savior. Stop running to scripture intended for un-redeemed and clever-in-their-own-mind sinners and instead—run to the verses where God is telling you what Christ has done for you and what He has re-made you to be. Run to verses that magnify the grace of God! God's wrath *no longer abides upon you*.

Walk in the new, completely. Affirm and establish, once and for all time, who God says that you are and why it is so! God gets the glory. He loves you! He re-created you! It's all because of grace, and this is a 5-letter word which carries enormous weight with it.

Your victory depends upon Jesus. Jesus has the victory. Jesus lives in you. Jesus doesn't live in sinners. Sinners practice sin and are slaves to sin. Jesus lives in sons. Sons practice righteousness and are slaves to righteousness.[27] You are righteous because of Jesus. You well know you are saved by grace, through faith in Jesus.

Therefore, walk in this victory! Never forget *you are who God says you are*, and not who you once were. God remembers your sins no more. Walk in this. You are *One New Dude!*

Then he says, "I will never again remember their sins and lawless deeds."
~Hebrews 10:17

The "Flesh"

As you are further exposed to your true identity by the Spirit of God, it might help to zero in on an important word the Bible uses. The word is, *"flesh."*

If you are to walk as *One New Dude*, you have to at least be willing to entertain different angles when it comes to certain parts or terms in scripture. Otherwise, you might be forever locked into the first thing you hear and learn. It might hold you back from all God has for you. Even Pastors in the pulpit share word studies from the originally used language in an attempt to clarify what the writer and ultimately God is conveying to us. They will also consider other commentators, which most likely are Bible scholars and teachers.

When it came to this word, *"flesh"*, I ended up getting confused about the whole *sinful nature* thing. I can't be alone on this. It's hard not to get confused. That is unless you swallow and accept everything you are taught, each and every time. We are commanded to test all things. Scripture can defend itself, right? How do you know God isn't calling you into a deeper understanding of his truth about your identity? When things don't seem to quite match up as you take into consideration God's *full* counsel, it's time to dig deeper.

For me, things stopped matching up when God told me my flesh was *already crucified,* as a recipient of grace and *truster* of Jesus Christ. When I stopped rushing past those verses which told me the old "I" *was indeed dead,* faith reached a whole new level of demand. Things didn't seem quite as comfortable as they once had, when it came to my trusting or not trusting what God was telling me.

When Paul said *he didn't live*—but it was Christ who lived in him—I began to have to deal more closely with this *death of self* aspect. You have to do the same in order to walk in God's newness for your life. God gives you grace to conform to his truth, so accept this grace. Also, consider not to do it at the expense of his truth.

Tell me, *One New Dude*: What good is God's truth if I don't believe Him and take Him at his Word?

Oh, I'm sure God's truth is *good* because *God is good!* Please don't misinterpret or misunderstand the question. It's rhetorical and it's an exhortation. *"What good is it?"* is the question? What good is God's gift of salvation, for example, if I don't accept it? What good is food if I don't eat it? Do you see? Why would Jesus go through all of this trouble if I never cash in on it? Doesn't He want me to know Him and to walk in the *actual and complete newness* He has secured for me, as *One New Dude*?

In the Original

Greek to English
sarx: flesh[28]

A short definition of this word does not get too specific. It's defined simply as *"flesh, body."*

A slightly longer definition includes the above, also adding to the mix, *"human nature."*

Together, you have what I would count as two options when substituting for this term from the original.

Those are: *1.) body 2.) human nature.*

In order to walk as *One New Dude*, I have discovered it's vital to continue studying in specific areas which yield revelation about your true identity.

This conceded, what we'll continue to try to do is gain a better understanding of the *flesh* while still simplifying things as much as possible. If this seems like a lot of extra work I would offer: so is lifting weights to build muscle mass. So is weeding the garden. This is your identity, Dude. I'm on your team! What's more, God is *for* you! It's worth digging into this. God instructs us to study to show thyself approved, so let's continue our investigation and journey of discovery! My hope is the time you take considering what is being presented in this book will have a tremendous impact on your life.

Anything that impacts your understanding of identity, especially with regard to any threat towards it, is being thrown into the spotlight. This is not for the faint of heart. If you want to settle for less than what God is giving, you can always avoid opportunities to trust what God is *really* saying in scripture.

However, this is not you, Dude. You are reading this book for a reason! That would be to establish once and for all an increasing awareness of v*ictory! It is also to establish a singular, liberating awareness* regarding who you actually are, in Jesus. That's what hangs in the balance.

Are you ready to continue? *Let's get back to it! Jesus is crazy about you!*

Humanness

We see the *flesh* used in two ways in the Bible. It can be used in a *moral or ethical* sense, as well as in a *physical* sense.

One Bible teacher I admire along with many others—John MacArthur—equates the *flesh* with a term he refers to as, *humanness*. This *humanness* would include the mind, body and emotions of a regenerated person.[29] Scripture always refers to the *unredeemed physical body* when speaking of the *flesh* in a moral or ethical sense.[30] It also carries with it an evil connotation when used in this same sense.[31]

Hopefully, you can see how splitting things up in a tidy way isn't always the easiest thing to do when investigating the *flesh*. God has made you as a complex creature, even *before* you were born again. When you add to the mix *being born again* and re-created, the level of complexity in assigning a *tidy* place to all things involved tends to dramatically increase.

Not to worry, though. God's grace is bigger than any problem-solving venture you or I may embark upon!

What this observation about *humanness* should do for us though, is further establish and remind us of where we get our identity. This side of heaven you will always be faced with the fact you have an unredeemed body which awaits redemption. You should simultaneously be reminded: while the promise is secured as a future event, your current reality is one of a redeemed *former sinner* who is now *One New Dude* and a *son of the Most High!* You have already been redeemed. Don't forget it!

Recognize no matter how scholars slice and dice when it comes to defining the *flesh*, your identity and nature depend solely upon God's Spirit. Adopting the definition we have cited for *humanness* or *flesh*, we can see a portion of it would include *parts* which comprise the soul. Those *parts* would be your mind and your emotions.

Why is this important? Some, which may or may not include yourself, might feel now is the time to jump in and conclude, *"There's your sinful nature, right there! What else would you call that?"*

Yet, don't forget so quickly. If you are to be consistent with the rest of scripture, it's extremely helpful to make a distinction between the *unredeemed physical body* and the *old man*. Notice how you had an *unredeemed physical body (flesh, humanness)* when you were not yet regenerated by the Holy Spirit. As the old self, your innermost[32] self—who was spiritually dead—occupied your *unredeemed physical body*.

Now however, as *One New Dude*, you still occupy this unredeemed physical body. The difference is *your nature has changed!* You were transformed!

It is fair to note Paul does admit *flesh* or *humanness* is still present—as we consider certain portions of scripture.[33]

Although, if one's definition or translation of *flesh* is *sinful nature*, then this is likely where some confusion and disagreement seem to creep in amongst Bible-believing Christians. Possibly, *double-nature* adopters reason *humanness (mind, emotions, body)* must automatically equate to what is known as man's *sinful nature*.

Conversely, *single-nature* proponents can make further distinctions regarding the *flesh*. This is not only because of the obvious *key-turning verses*, but also perhaps because of translation differences. As you will see in some of the upcoming examples, *flesh* is used instead of *sinful nature* in *at least one earlier Bible translation*. This is not a small thing.

As the *old man* your flesh *was not crucified*. Therefore, your old man still existed. As the *One New Dude*, your flesh *was crucified supernaturally*. A tremendous gift from God! Therefore, your old man no longer exists. Perhaps in your mind he does. This is where you'll need to change your mind. Your nature and identity determine if sin *reigns* or if sin only *survives*. As *One New Dude* sin merely *survives*; it no longer *reigns*.

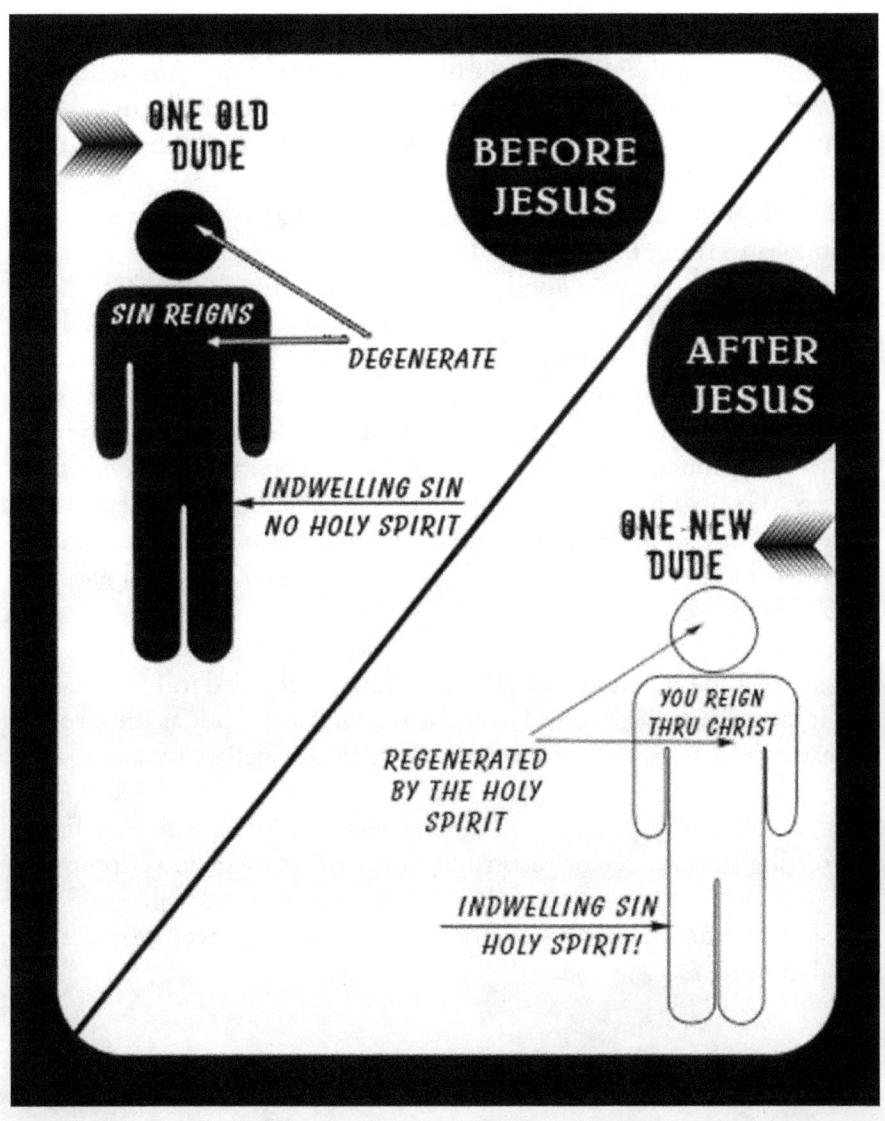

You might reasonably conclude the Lord uses *surviving* sin, along with his indwelling Spirit, for the good of your intimate relationship with Him. If so, I wouldn't disagree with you. God can use the surviving cancer of sin to establish a deeper, loving dependency upon Him. Intimate communion with God is how it all started for man! You were created to walk intimately with your Creator, but you had to find your way to Him, through Jesus. *Hallelujah, once again!*

In any case, do you see those distinctions which were just

made and why they are important? When you take the narrow road—which is making the difficult but necessary distinctions surrounding the *flesh*—you end up *without* a sinful nature and *without* a sinful identity. Why? It's because the *old man has been crucified,* according to God.

Remember: it isn't because you just decided one day it was a good idea to think this way. It's because you decided *(or hopefully will decide)* one day—it was a good idea to think this way *because God revealed to you* this is the *real One New Dude!* The *One New Dude* He had recreated you to be... the whole way through!

Understand and accept this: Your soul is being restored as *One New Dude.* God can do what He desires.[34] He can establish you as *new* while simultaneously walking with you as you *uncover, discover and conform* to his truth you are *new.* Having a soul that is being healed and instructed by God does not necessitate your *humanness* defines your nature or identity. To the contrary, *God's Holy Spirit determines your nature and identity.*

If God wanted a *sinful nature* to remain as a piece of the puzzle for the *One New Dude,* He would have included it. He chose not to include it. *Hallelujah!* He chose do the hard work at the Cross, in Jesus, then allow for you to participate in the victory by *turning the key.*

Still, we'll continue to examine this term, *flesh.* You may find it interesting to consider or reconsider some of its usage in scripture, as well as its implications in your life. When more carefully analyzed for the sake of true identity discovery, I promise you it's well worth it. On that note, *let's keep moving!*

*"**S**alvation is not a matter of improvement or perfection of what has previously existed. It is total transformation. At the new birth a person becomes `a new creature; the old things passed away; behold, new things have come' (2 Cor. 5:17). It is not simply that he receives something new but that he becomes someone new. The new nature is not added to the old nature but replaces it. The transformed person is a completely new `I'. Biblical terminology, then, does not say that a Christian has two different natures. He has but one nature, the new nature in Christ. The old self dies and the new self lives; they do not coexist. It is not a remaining old nature but the remaining garment of sinful flesh that causes Christians to sin. The Christian is a single new person, a totally new creation, not a spiritual schizophrenic. The believer as a total person is transformed but not yet wholly perfect. He has residing sin but no longer reigning sin. He is no longer the old man corrupted but is now the new man created in righteousness and holiness, awaiting full salvation."* (Taken from The MacArthur New Testament Commentary-EPHESIANS, p. 164 © 1986 by John MacArthur. Used with permission of Moody Publishers.)

Translations & Perspectives

In this *One New Dude* discovery process, why is it important Bible translation can change perspectives, where the term *"flesh"* is concerned?

Let me state right up front any criticism of the popular translations of the Bible should not be used as ammunition to discredit them. I am honored we have robust translations which make it easier to grasp the meaning of God's eternal word. An occasional observation regarding some tricky translation challenges, at least from my end, should not be interpreted as my discrediting or disparaging Bible translations, in general. This is not my intention, nor do I carry any credentials to be taken seriously would I ever attempt to do such a thing. I have no *formal* training or education when it comes to textual criticism, seminary, or even Bible College—at least, not at the time of writing this book of encouragement to you.

Regardless, as a Spirit-filled believer and like any Spirit-filled believer who is studying the Word, certain situations that demand clarity come up as we seek the Lord. You can appeal to two Bible teachers, both having multiple degrees and years and years of Bible teaching under their belts, and they may give you two different viewpoints and positions, regarding one specific topic.

As much as I had hoped everything would be *tidy* and nothing would ever need to be debated, this simply is not the case when studying certain areas of scripture. Someone once said, likely referring to discussion or debate amongst Christians, *"Unity in the essentials, and liberty in the non-essentials."*

For example, some *essentials* might be:

- Jesus is God in flesh.
- Jesus was born of a virgin.
- Man desperately needs a Savior and his name is Jesus.

When we get into *non-essential* matters, *liberty* is the exhortation. I like this. *Liberty on non-essentials* strikes me as a wise proposal. As scripture teaches, see to it you do not *devour* each other. Do all things with love. Even when we fail to love, forgive. This kind of attitude pleases God. The Spirit of Christ must reign amongst us, even as challenging topics are examined.

Suffice it to say, there is a battle going on. Only, it's not a battle that includes a *sinful nature*, which is your *old self*. Rather, the *battle* involves the Holy Spirit and your *unredeemed physical body*.

God's *One New Dude* plan is much better to me than some type of *Fragmented Dude* plan. With this plan you can and will still fall short at times. However, you are not confused about who you are as a result. There is a place allocated to the source of sin but it's not another nature or person within you.

You have *one* identity as a partaker of the divine nature. Christ lives, not the old you, if you belong to Jesus. Therefore, if you fall short in thought or action you know very well God makes you aware of this inconsistency with who you are in Christ. You recognize it's contrary to your nature and you simply agree you need to change your mind about it.

This is why I suggest the more you realize and dare I say—*finally accept who you are* and *who you are not*—the less likely you will excuse actions or thoughts contrary to your divine nature. You should become less comfortable and hopefully entirely *uncomfortable* attributing anything unwholesome you might say or do to some *dual* personality. That old dude's dead. Anything like this goes where the Bible assigns it. I attempt to illustrate this to you within the pages of this book.

Believe me. As far as essentials and non-essentials go, I'm not ready to say where one stands on the *sinful nature's* existence for the believer is a *non-essential*.

Nonetheless, in the Spirit of Christ—it would be wise to extend grace to one another. What we are considering is not trivial, by a long-shot! This is a true identity matter. We have incredible revelation which exhorts each of us into a new life, as a *new creation*. God has spoken and is still speaking to those who have ears to hear. Are you one of them?

Drawing Distinctions

A good illustration of how various translations might lead to confusion over the term *"flesh"* is as follows. Let's just browse through them, briefly:

1. For if you live according to the **sinful nature**, you will die; but if by the Spirit you put to death the **misdeeds** of the **body**, you will live, ~ **Romans 8:13 NIV**

2. For if you live by **its dictates**, you will die. But if through the power of the Spirit you put to death the **deeds** of your **sinful nature**, you will live. ~ **Romans 8:13 NLT**

   Notice here, above. You have one translation interpreting *"flesh"* as *"sinful nature,"* the other interpreting *"flesh"* as *"body."* Also interesting to observe is how closely aligned but still distinct the two are from each other.

You are being offered reasonable evidence—in this book—it's helpful to make distinctions. It's important they are made, if you are to walk as *One New Dude*. God made the distinctions; why shouldn't we? He indicates in scripture: 1.) your sinful nature was crucified 2.) you are new 3.) still, you must *finish this race* with an unredeemed physical body.

Distinctions need to be made. Citing how translations differ should heighten your awareness on this matter of the term, *"flesh."*

3. "for if you are living according to the **flesh**, you must die; but if by the Spirit you are putting to death the **deeds** of the ***body***, you will live." ~ **Romans 8:13 NASB**

Look at this one, above: *"Flesh"* is left alone, in its original Greek-to-English translation. What comes after this mention of the *flesh*? A reference to the *deeds* of what? Correct! The deeds of the *physical body*. Your physical body is a liability. It is what carries sin's cancer.

Let me strongly suggest you *not allow* anyone to corner you into submitting to something God has not necessarily revealed for you to submit to. Your physical body carrying the cancer of sin, until it's redeemed, does not require God expects for you to carry around your old identity as a sinner. Granted, it would do unsaved people well to know they are sinners and need a Savior, but you already knew this. This is why you received Christ! You need not fall in line with any teaching which over-emphasizes sin—once you become a son. If you want to you can. However, as you look at scripture and what Jesus has done, do you really think God wants you identified as anything *old?*

Understand: Your identity is at stake! If you choose to be passive when it comes to peer pressure regarding your identity, you will sacrifice it upon an altar God never intended. Let this never be. God is good! Praise Him right now! Thank You, Jesus! Eyes are being opened to the *fullness* of Your grace. *Hallelujah!*

Based upon the previously shared *original* definition, it seems reasonable to conclude translators decide which word or phrase is chosen to substitute for the term, *"flesh"*, when *"flesh"* is *not* used. With all of the biblical evidence pointing to a *crucified and buried old-self (identity)* or *sinful nature*, it should be *reasonable* to examine the sin liability which remains with the *physical body*.

This I would offer is more consistent and helpful in recognizing the *sinful nature* is no more. Since the *divine nature* is what defines your singular identity and nature, the *One New Dude* should seriously consider scriptural opportunities which allow for distinctions to be made regarding the *old self* versus the *unredeemed physical body*.

OK, so let's do the first one using *"sinful nature"* in the place of *"flesh"*. **This is strictly for examination purposes:**

> "for if you are living according to the **old-self/sinful nature**, you must die; but if by the Spirit you are putting to death the **deeds** of the **body**, you will live."
> **~ Romans 8:13 edited NASB**
> Scripture taken from the NEW AMERICAN STANDARD BIBLE(r),
> (c) Copyright 1960, 1962, 1963, 1968, 1971, 1972, 1973, 1975, 1977, 1995
> by The Lockman Foundation Used by permission. (www.Lockman.org)

Verse Comments: When we use this interpretive option, versus the *"physical body"* option, it clearly holds true. It's clear the *degenerate* or *unregenerate* dude is going to die. For, there is no life of Christ within this dude. No disagreement, here.

That said, this does not seem to necessitate that the other option of the **physical body** is a poor choice for a substitution option (in this post-fall case, *an "unredeemed" physical body*), especially in light of what is known regarding the localization of sin in one's *members*.

Next, let's just see how things play out using the *physical body* option. **This is also strictly for examination purposes:**

> "for if you are living according to the **unredeemed physical body**, you must die; but if by the Spirit you are putting to death the **deeds** of the **body**, you will live."
> **~ Romans 8:13 edited NASB**
> Scripture taken from the NEW AMERICAN STANDARD BIBLE(r),

(c) Copyright 1960, 1962, 1963, 1968, 1971, 1972, 1973, 1975, 1977, 1995 by The Lockman Foundation Used by permission. (www.Lockman.org)

One more translation helps us even further, and has this verse as:

> "For if you live by **its dictates**, you will die. But if through the power of the Spirit you put to death the **deeds** of your **sinful nature**, you will live."
> ~ **Romans 8:13 NLT**

"But wait!" you might say. It says right there: *"sinful nature!"* I warned you this can be confusing based upon how *"flesh"* is interpreted. Everybody is in agreement living by the sinful nature leads to death. This has been established.

What's currently being investigated is how *"flesh"* is being interpreted, and how it can provide reasonable evidence the *physical body*—being the *base of operation for sin*—is still a viable option for translating or interpreting *flesh*. An old, sinful nature should no longer be given any accommodation when describing the *One New Dude*. God certainly isn't giving it any reason to be *alive* or to *hang around*. Why would you?

It's so worth *seeking and finding*—for your very identity is at stake! How much would the enemy of your soul celebrate over you never discovering who you are, after Jesus paid such a high price for you to come into a discovery of it?

Jesus Drew Distinctions

You remember this one, right? As a youngster, you might have heard this as you learned about the hours leading up to Christ's crucifixion.

> **JESUS:** *"Watch and pray so that you will not fall into temptation. The spirit is willing, but the body is weak."*
> ~ **Mark 14:38 NIV**

Here, Jesus also gives us some evidence *the body* is a liability, when it comes to *"willing"* to do the right thing. It's weak. It has the cancer of sin.

On temptation to sin, He actually has something *good* to say when speaking of the spirit, but *not-so-good* to say when it comes to the frail, human body. The great news for you is God the Holy Spirit has made you new because He now indwells you, as a believer.

In God's Kingdom—this includes all things true—1+1+1=1.[35] Three distinct *ones*, yet still *one*. God the Father, God the Son, God the Holy Spirit. One God.

Likewise, you are body, soul and spirit. 1+1+1=1. Three, yet one. Splitting these aspects of your being is critical for you to understand who you are.

"The Word became flesh."
~ John 1:14

God becoming a Man… Jesus was Spirit-filled, has a soul, and has a body.

"Flesh" here only refers to a *body*. So, you can see *flesh* isn't necessarily required to be linked to a sinful nature. I just wanted to cite one example so that you don't feel you must automatically equate *"flesh"* with *sinful nature*. Jesus had no sin in Him, but He had/has *"flesh"*—a physical *body—wouldn't you agree?*

He does still have flesh according to what we know from Scripture. Remember when Jesus promised to come back and then ascended to heaven in bodily form? Look at this verse since we've stumbled upon it in discussing the *flesh:*

"Men of Galilee," they said, "why do you stand here looking into the sky? This same Jesus, who has been taken from you into heaven, will come back in the same way you have seen him go into heaven."
~ Acts 1:11

Even though Jesus became flesh and had a body, we know He had *neither sin* in his body's *"members,"* nor did He have a *sinful-nature*.

Flesh/Body = Weak

Let's look at it one more time with a parallel translation.

1. *"Watch and pray so that you will not fall into temptation. The spirit is willing, but the <u>body</u> is weak."*
~ **Mark 14:38 NIV**

2. *"Watch and pray that you may not enter into temptation. The spirit indeed is willing, but the <u>flesh</u> is weak."*
~ **Mark 14:38 ESV**

The above examples then provide insight regarding the *"flesh."* The word in these examples is being narrowed down to refer to the *body,* and *not necessarily the sinful nature.*

Please take this into consideration anytime you read scripture. Remember: *"flesh"* may or may not be referring to the *sinful nature* in certain areas of scripture. You can see such is not *always* and *necessarily* the case, based upon some of the examples presented within these pages.

Jesus is Strong!

You accepted Jesus in to fight the battles you were not capable of winning. His Spirit came in to save, seal and sanctify you. He came in to put to death anything *lurking* and *left over* which is from your *way of thought* when you had no spiritual life.

The sinful nature *once* operative in you but now crucified, used to constantly give into your body's sinful deeds. Christ is now in you to snuff those deeds out and bring you home. The Lord is a Warrior and He lives in you! Praise the King! God has exhorted lovingly that you offer to Him the members of your body. That you would live fully devoted to Him! You cooperate with God by deciding it makes good sense to present the members of your body — which are riddled with the cancer of sin—to Him.

When it seems to be too much, talk to Him! Invest in your relationship with Him. He knows what's going on. He knows what the plan *was* and *is*. He's *for you!* Cast your cares upon Him for He cares for you!

Nailing Down the Flesh

No, we're not talking *crucifying your flesh* with the title above. If you are a die hard, *"I'm gonna crucify my sinful nature every day"* kind of Christian, good try! This work is complete in the believer according to verses already cited. Instead, you are being provided with multiple and reasonable considerations which narrow down this term *"flesh"* so you can hold fast only to the good!

What made and can still make this so tricky is *"flesh"* isn't always understood so readily and so easily. Because the term has more than one possibility when it comes to being defined— and because those options can be so closely related—it's easy to lump both of them into one definition, using them interchangeably. In this case I'm referring to the *old man* versus the *physical body*.

The Bible however, when examined more in depth, causes us to stretch our understanding of where everything belongs. If it didn't directly impact your *true* identity, perhaps it wouldn't be such a big deal to sort out in such specific detail.

The fact of the matter though, is if you are to recognize Scripture for what God is saying, you're not always going to have man's approval. Consider Jesus. Consider Paul. They were both murdered. Consider Stephen and the other apostles who were murdered. Religious people are not always going to agree with you when you take God at his Word, then share it. Pure grace has always had a problem penetrating religious people. Many people claim to be doing God's work while obstructing the message of pure grace, whether intentionally or not.

Nicodemus seemed like a good man; one who loved God. Yet, Jesus delivered a mind-blowing message of grace that involved receiving a gift, not working for it. Nicodemus showed signs of receiving this while many others did not. *You're God's child, Dude! Jesus did all of the work!*

When God injects pure grace, man seems to have a bent towards watering it down. Pure grace, which continues to be revealed *after* the conversions of the converted, is so amazing it risks being *diluted.* Man has proven he oftentimes wills to work for salvation, even *after accepting* the gospel of grace!

You can also get a pulse if you were to survey people walking down the street: *"If you died tonight, would you go to heaven?"* You can observe them so often proclaim, *"Why yes! Why would I? Well because I'm a good person!"* Indicators prove man wants to work for at least some of it, whether it's intentionally or unintentionally. Converted souls attempting to battle an *old self* are served well in remaining vigilant, when it comes to works:

> *"Now to the <u>one who works</u>, <u>his wage is not credited as a favor</u>, but as what is due. 5But <u>to the one who does not work</u>, but believes in Him who justifies the ungodly, <u>his faith is credited as righteousness</u>,*
> *6just as David also speaks of the blessing on the man to whom God credits righteousness apart from works:*
> *7BLESSED ARE THOSE WHOSE LAWLESS DEEDS HAVE BEEN FORGIVEN,*
> *AND WHOSE SINS HAVE BEEN COVERED.*
> *8BLESSED IS THE MAN WHOSE SIN THE LORD WILL NOT TAKE INTO ACCOUNT."*
> **~ Romans 4 NASB**

Agreeing with the masses of born-again believers or trusting a specific teaching solely because popular teachers may hold this same view does not make a thing necessarily true. Each of us must concede this, including myself. *(To my knowledge, though, one-naturism or the single-natured viewpoint is currently far outnumbered by those who ascribe to a double-natured position.)*

Nevertheless, consider the Pharisees. Consider Saul before his conversion. These people were educated. Peter on the other hand… did not appear to be. He was a fisherman. Even so, God still uses Peter today to educate the *wise* of the world.

When Saul was converted and began going by Paul as he preached God's grace, the educated scoffed at him. Paul, on the other hand, was determined to *know nothing among them other than Jesus Christ and Him crucified,* even though he had plenty of credentials of which to make appeal. Numbers didn't appear to be on the side of Jesus when many shouted, *"Crucify Him!"* Yet, we know *Jesus was, is and always will be... the Truth.*

Believe what you believe because God has revealed it to you, not because the majority holds that view. The majority just could be wrong on a certain issue. Is this in the realm of possibility? They may even get most things right, and praise God for them! We need each other in the Body of Christ. Still, they are *fallible,* as are both you and I. God however, is *infallible.* If truth on a matter can be and should be known, God is happy to reveal it. You can know who you *are,* not who you *think* you are. You can know who you are according to God!

As stated before, when believers see things differently on a given matter, the Holy Spirit will guide them and you into all truth. Maybe the arguments presented in this book, which are intended for you to uncover and embrace your true identity, are incorrect.

However, maybe they are not. Maybe these ideas that lean upon the scriptures and revelation from God are actually accurate and just what God desired for you trust, today? Don't stop depending upon the Holy Spirit. The fear of man is a snare! God *has transformed you* and *is transforming* you now—that you would be conformed to the truth you actually *have been transformed.* What a Creator!

Don't fall into what I fell into, or don't stay where this is. I used to say to myself,

"Oh that makes complete sense! I sin here and I sin there and I do this thing over here because well, after all, that's my sinful nature that I'm in the process of putting it to death! The "two" of me are fighting and God's stronger than my sinful nature! There's a sort of boxing match between the two going on, right inside of my body. This is fierce, but my money's on the Holy Spirit and He's going to put to death that old man of mine. Get him, God!"

Actually, I can certainly see why some might think this way. It all seems to reason out until other portions of scripture are taken into account. As I see it—and perhaps you can find some solace in this, as well—Christians who debate this issue on nature are *not* really far apart in their respective views. Both love and live for Jesus. Both are members of the Body of Christ. We are one! This reality that the new creation is *incarcerated*[86] in unredeemed flesh is something both experience. Even so, how something is interpreted, dispensed and ultimately consumed obviously plays no small role in the matter.

If, in one of the views and by God's permission, you get to be rid of a major hindrance *(i.e. a sinful nature)* but in the other you do not, it's kind of a big deal—wouldn't you say?

Contrary to the specific details of an *old man* fighting in the battle described above, we know the Bible tells us *Jesus has already dealt with my old man*, so I wouldn't have to. It was a gift. *Amazing Grace! Hallelujah!* This most certainly applies to you as *One New Dude!* It's available to anyone who will humble themselves to receive *all* of God's grace.

By the way, I'm not speaking for anyone but myself when I recount my private reasoning. This used to be my experience. It was troubling and caused identity issues of which I have not re-visited since *turning the key*. If you happen to relate to what I'm saying then you know the *deal*.

I also can only begin to tell you how my walk changed immediately and how it continues to change for the better. It's all because my identity crisis is over. It's as if God gave me my identity crisis to find my way out of it and encourage you to do the same. *Knowing your true identity* will give you victory like you've *never known* before.

In times of trials and temptation, being settled and persuaded regarding my true nature and identity resolves the crisis. I would suggest you can only be settled and persuaded on your identity if you *turn the key* on God's key-turning verses, which were previously shared. Establishing ahead of time what is important is wise and will pay off time and time again as you journey through your new life in Jesus, as *One New Dude*.

Hopefully, this closer examination of the flesh has reduced the amount of comfort you may have had or still carry when considering the sinful nature. If I hadn't believed God was ratcheting up the pressure in my own life—as far as what I trusted or didn't trust when it came to my true identity—I wouldn't be encouraging you into a more careful examination of it within your own life. The time has been well invested for me and I pray it is for you, as well.

Got Buckets?

They say a cluttered desk is a cluttered mind. If this is true then I would offer it will benefit you —as a Christian—to have some *buckets* to organize your thinking. These bucket assignments will hopefully augment your efforts in *location assignment*, both for what *Jesus has accomplished* and for what *God has revealed,* as it relates to you!

So… what do you say we assign some *buckets* to help us get organized? Allow me to propose four of those for you to consider. You might consider adopting these as your own if it's helpful to you. As you continue to be washed by the water of the Word, you will likely find no view is perfectly *tidy*, and this is because even Bible scholars differ on what goes where.

Nevertheless, examining more carefully what the Bible teaches is never a bad thing, is it? The secret things may belong to God but He loves revealing Himself to us, if we'd simply *ask, seek and knock.* We may not fully understand everything which is revealed but if you're like me, you're happy to take what the Master's handing out. Certainly, the lady who was rewarded for her faith illustrates God approves when we humble ourselves and persist. She said to Jesus:

> *"but even the dogs under the table eat the children's crumbs."*
> **~ Mark 7:29 NIV**

Finally, as you do consider the other views out there, I would offer the means of organizing and assigning what goes where—as is written in this book—is offered in faith. I have sought guidance and counsel from the Holy Spirit. I have asked God to help me know what my true identity is in Christ. In this process of discovery, I am compelled to share my experience. I desire to help others know their identity as I believe God wants you to know what your true identity is, as well! After all, you are *One New Dude* and you need to know this every minute of every day!

The *contents* of the various buckets can be used interchangeably with bucket labels when referencing. This is an imperfect attempt to add some clarity to your thinking:

Bucket for the "Deceased or Replaced" - *Contents:* *"Flesh":* *sin nature/old-self/old-man, depraved mind, stony heart, filthy rags, flesh deeds, sin.*

Bucket for the "Soon-To-Be-Deceased" - *Contents:* *"Flesh":* *physical unredeemed body, humanness, flesh deeds, sin.* A body not yet glorified but promised glorification/perfection. *Humanness*[37] includes mind, body, & emotions. We touch more on this, shortly!

Bucket for the "Existing" - *Contents:* *Divine nature/Holy Spirit, mind of Christ, heart of flesh, the gift of righteousness, new man, flesh deeds, sin.*

Bucket for the "Coming Soon" - *Contents:* *Redeemed body, Perfection*

Whether we *believe* something is true doesn't necessarily make it true, isn't that right?

For example, when you talk to an atheist, them simply not believing God exists or Mormons not believing Jesus is the eternal God incarnate or so on and so forth… does not make a thing true, right? Of course it doesn't. Thank goodness for that! You can believe all kinds of things, but believing a thing is not what makes it true, or not.

God has spoken in more than one verse above. Someone/something died. He's pointing to the *sin nature*, or the *old self*, or the *old man*. We can listen, believe God and *benefit*; can we not? Yes! I would propose a resounding, *"Yes!"* Of course you can!

You should be encouraged today by what Jesus has done. He has set you free from your sinful nature! Just because you sin at times doesn't mean you have two natures or identities opposed to each other. You have an unredeemed body and are a new creation. There are not two people inside of you, an old and a new. God has re-made you! God is *for* blessing you! He demonstrates this… how? In that, He did not spare his only Son! Why would God promote and reveal your old self/sin nature is dead if He wanted you to keep giving it any thought—or to think in your mind it still has anything to do with your identity?

You need to let go of this flawed way of thinking. If you recall, Satan struck right at the center of Christ's identity, when he began to tempt Him. Satan said, *"If you are the Son of God…"*[38]

If Satan can be effective at taking the rug out from underneath you by deceiving you about your identity—and all of this before you even get started dealing with whatever the temptation is at hand—then how will you walk in truth, authority and victory? This doesn't need to be how your story goes. The Lord is working with you about identity. Let Him have his way. *Hallelujah to the Lion who reigns!*

Accounting for Sin

You might ask: *"How can I then account for sin as a new creation, if there's no sin nature?"*

I'm glad you might be asking this. It involves a combination of the following, I would suggest.

Indwelling sin: We know sin, *even in the believer*, dwells within the *members* of the *unredeemed flesh/body*. Notice this *"flesh"* is *not* synonymous with your identity as *One New Dude*. Rather, the sin cancer is in the body you occupy until it's redeemed with another body; a redeemed body.

Identity Conformation: The distance between who you believe you are and who God says you are in Christ should *decrease* along the believer's journey of *sanctification*. In this case, your journey! One way of defining sanctification might be: the distance between being born-again *(regenerated, justified)* and being *glorified*.

The combination of these things could offer a reasonable explanation as to why a new creation can still sin without having a sin nature. If you think you are always bent towards sin rather than bent towards righteousness, of what will your mind and behavior gravitate towards most? What does God want you to be bent towards now—as a *new creation*, not of the *crucified* old man? Does God want you to focus on being a *slave to sin* or a *slave to righteousness? Old self* or *new self? Sin nature* or *divine nature?* Who lives? You say, *"Cristo!"*

Why would Jesus go through so much at the cross—as well as to tell you the sin nature is already crucified in his Word—if He wanted you to consider it to be alive? Does He desire your precious time, energy and focus be spent worrying about something which has already been dealt with by his grace? Or, is He quite serious about you accepting who He says *you now are*, in Christ?

Now, you may already be familiar with this basic reality of *justification, sanctification and glorification* in the believer's life. That's terrific and it wouldn't surprise me in the least if you've been studying and seeking. If you've been sitting at the feet of Jesus your mind is being renewed, to be sure.

Yet, what I am proposing is this. *(Please avoid proof-texting.)*

If—along this journey of sanctification a proper understanding of who God says you are is never trusted or believed to be true—couldn't this easily have a significant impact on how you walk out the rest of your Christian life? Couldn't that prolong this area of your sanctification, as it relates to your true identity?

In other words, if God has emphasized on more than one occasion the old man or sin nature was handled by Jesus at the cross, *but instead* you walk as if it *wasn't* dealt with, your outlook is going to be different than it would be if you trusted what He says; will it not? What if the *key was turned*, instead? It's not as if most or any of us *turn the key* right on time every time, right? God is patient with us, oftentimes waiting for us to embrace all aspects of truth. Nevertheless, the key needs to be turned, doesn't it?

There's a bucket labeled, *"Deceased"*. Your sin nature resides in this bucket according to the Bible. It's your old self. That person is dead as far as God is concerned. If you belong to Jesus and have accepted his sacrifice—you have then *already crucified* that old nature when you accepted Him and received your salvation *package*.

Sanctification is the primary *arena* where the believer struggles with sin. It's not the source of sin, of course. This is not what is being presented. What Jesus has done and what God has said—intersecting a forgiven sinner's heart, mind and body—is going to shake things up a bit. It's going to turn things upside down which is actually right-side up. Within this shake-up or *transformation*, old thinking is being replaced by new thinking. You are reaching forward to lay hold of what Christ laid hold of you for; perfection! Christ has already made perfect those who are being sanctified!

In order for you to make some sense out of why—while you don't practice sin you still may fall short at times—it's helpful to have a place for it. It cannot be in your already crucified sin nature. You need to get this phrase *in check* as a believer and partaker of the divine nature.

If your body attempts to rise up, Jesus helps you to beat it back because you submit to Him as Lord, right? If you fail on occasion—in thought or deed—you have an Advocate to plead your case: Jesus and his blood. Don't succumb to identity lies and lose faith. Cast the lies down. He lives, you don't. He's working in you, He's bringing you along. God is faithful to complete his work. Your soul is catching up to God's miracle in you; it's all good! Don't panic.

With all due respect to my brothers and sisters who might hold to an alternate view, it's just not consistent with what God has revealed to give any power or authority to an already crucified nature. We'll want to respect each other if we are to remain obedient to Jesus. Let us patiently examine and ponder our reasons as we stand upon God's Word. You'll never have another door opened if you don't feel you ever need to knock again, right? Jesus articulated you are to, *"Ask, seek, and knock."* You're not done with this, are you? God has more for you!

In the Spirit of Christ, let's continue to *ask, seek, and knock*. You will be persuaded the old man or sin nature is dead and buried already, or you will not. If God can't convince you, I certainly cannot.

Nevertheless, many Christians are likely hungry for this breakthrough in their understanding. *"What exactly did Christ accomplish on my behalf?"* You may not even know you are looking for this, and this is why I believe God has placed me into your path—to draw your attention to it.

Father, fill each of us with Your Spirit. Keep our eyes fixed upon Jesus as we extend brotherly love towards one another. Continue to unite us as one in Spirit, regardless of potential differing opinions. In Christ's good name, amen.

As the new creation you are, it's reasonable for you to pursue just what Jesus has done on your behalf. It would be terrific to do so while accepting fully what God has revealed to us. It's reasonable to desire for everything to have its proper place. It's good to be organized. God is not the author of confusion, amen?

God wants you to experience what it is to be *undivided*—operating as one, divine-natured re-creation of the Most High—fully filled with His Spirit! Appreciating and accepting biblically consistent reasoning as it relates to your nature can help you trust what God says about your true identity.

Assigning Sin's Proper Place

There are three verses which can assist you in assigning sin to its proper place. Be encouraged. You don't need to hold a view which causes you to contradict other verses, simultaneously causing confusion about who you truly are, in Jesus.

As illustrated above, when you like Paul, find yourself doing what you don't want to do—it can't be *you* who is doing it. Why? Paul already stated you are dead. God shows us through Paul there's a specific *law or principle* to single out as the source: this source is *sin!* Not an old man or sinful nature, but the *dreaded cancer of sin*, itself!

"*So now, no longer am I the one doing it, but sin which dwells in me.*"
~ **Romans 7:17 NASB**

Now, I also want you to recognize to an even further degree how God has narrowed the source of sin residing in your unredeemed flesh, which is your unredeemed physical body. Let's analyze this verse a bit so you can zero in on what is being revealed to us, by the Lord.

"For I know that <u>nothing good</u> dwells in me, that is, in my flesh;"
~ **Romans 7:18 NASB**

Exhortation:
"nothing good" = sin
"in my flesh" = physical, unredeemed body
Conclusion: Sin *lurks* in the physical, unredeemed body.

It's not all bad news on your unredeemed body, though. Even though sin resides there, your unredeemed body can be used for good! The *One New Dude* offers the members of his flesh/body to God as a living sacrifice. You know you are *One New Dude* because the old dude wasn't interested in presenting his body as a living sacrifice to God; only to sin. You *can perform* and *are called to good works*, being in Christ. Understand you *are* reigning because *He is reigning* over sin in your body. You died, He lives. It's the ultimate package.

At the same time, God tells us until you get this new, redeemed body—the *cancer of sin* still finds its dwelling place within the *members* of your physical body.

As *One New Dude*, you have dominion over sin because Christ broke its power in your life and his Spirit lives in you. *Hallelujah!* Do you believe it? Believe it! It's a huge shift from where you once were to where you now are, in Him.

"for the willing is present in me, but the doing of the good is not. For the good that I want, I do not do, but I practice the very evil that I do not want."
~ **Romans 7:18b, 19 NASB**

As *One New Dude*, you are increasingly more sensitive to sin in the sense you know you are a partaker in the divine nature. You are no longer ruled by a sinful nature. *(Your soul needs to learn this.)*

This is normal for the spiritually alive in Christ. Just because

Paul wrestles with the fact he doesn't always do the good he desires, it does *not* mean Paul *never does any good.* To the contrary! Paul was persecuting Christians. Now, he's being used by God to write a big chunk of the New Testament! Kind of a good thing and a big shift, is it not? Lots of good things! There are mostly good things and rarely bad things as compared with the previous life and old self. Don't mistake Paul's humility for some type of helpless, hopeless sinner doomed to be a slave to sin. It is not consistent with the other things he said.

As *One New Dude*, yes…you have some *fallout* from who you once were. You might categorize the fallout as *"wounds-suffered-needing-healing"* and *"wrong-thinking-needing-correcting."* God's bigger. Do not fear. Your Savior Jesus is victorious and He lives in you!

Furthermore, God's grace is still empowering you to be conformed to his truth about you. Compared to Christ in you, whatever *fallout* you are being restored from isn't the big story. *Jesus is!* The *One New Dude* who results *is* because sin is defeated and you are *now* reigning, through Christ! *As Jesus is in heaven so are you on the earth!* Having confidence for the Day of Judgment impacts how you live today: free! You must place the emphasis where God intends for it to be, and it's not on sin! It's on righteousness. Praise the King!

> *"But if I am doing the very thing I do not want, <u>I am no longer the one doing it</u>, <u>but sin which dwells in me.</u>"*
> **~ Romans 7:20 NASB**

When you are re-created it is impossible to actually raise from the dead your old self. You might be able to trick yourself into it but it wouldn't coincide with truth. It forces you to believe you actually *still do live* and not Christ, alone. Do you see why turning the key is so critical? God isn't interested in you gaining *man's approval* regarding what He says *is or isn't the case* on a certain matter. He's interested in you trusting it simply because He said it. That's awesome because who is more trustworthy than God?

Once more, God through Paul tells us the source of sin. It's not Paul's sinful nature because we know this has been cut away, crucified and buried. We know Christ handled this at the cross from Colossians 2:11, amongst other passages.

God instructs you the cancer of *"sin"* itself is *"doing it"*—that is, *"the very thing"* Paul doesn't want to do!

This doesn't remove the responsibility of you possessing your vessel in sanctification and honor. *You most certainly are responsible.* You are the once-practicing-sinner who was saved by grace and have become a son and a saint! Being responsible for possessing your vessel (in sanctification and honor) is nothing to fear, though. Why? It's because you are not relying upon your old self or a dead sinful nature to take home the victory. Your faith is in the *One* who indwells you. The *Spirit of Christ!* It's the *Spirit of Christ* who causes you to **be** *One New Dude!*

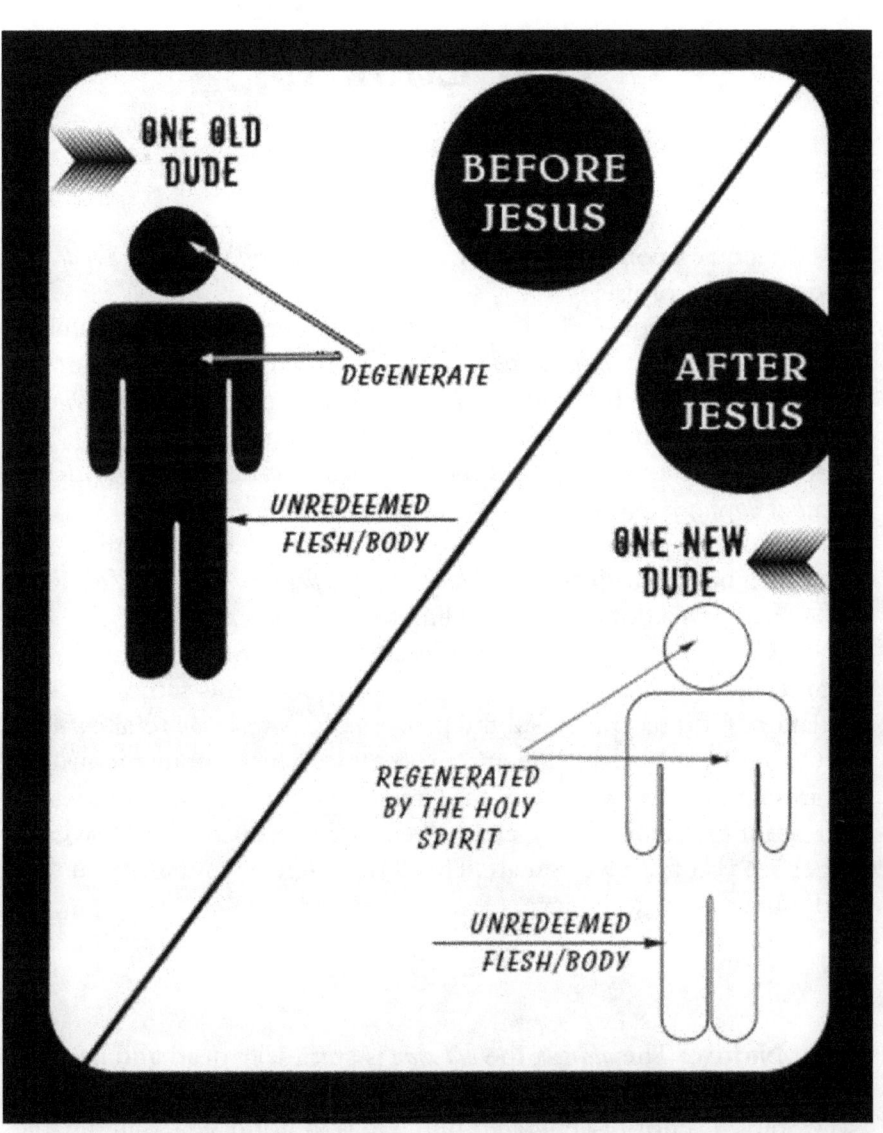

You Lookin' at Me?

Let's do a quick comparison of the *old dude* and the *One New Dude*. It's good news, I promise!

In the believer, the *One New Dude* <u>replaces</u> the One Old Dude. It isn't *addition*, it's *transformation*—both at the time of conversion, as well as throughout the process of sanctification. The *One New Dude* undergoes a continual process: *"sanctification."* This progressively conforms the *One New Dude* to the true reality of his identity which God *has already declared.*

For our purposes, what God has already declared is this: those who belong to Jesus *have crucified* their *flesh/sinful nature/old self/old man*. It's a done deal regarding the *old you.*

Once more, because this is eternal revelation from the Creator, the *One New Dude* must *digest* and process this same revelation. God has provided the process of *sanctification* to allow for the *One New Dude's* digesting and processing, which simultaneously requires an ongoing trust with his Creator. As a loving parent sees their beautiful but doubting child, even more so does your Heavenly Father see you for who you are. He all the while encourages you to *not* doubt and *only* to believe.

"old dude"

Sinful Nature: The *old-self*, the *old man* is spiritually dead and has no power over sin. He is a *"Death-Walker."* He is degenerate as God's Holy Spirit has not re-generated him. He is in bondage to sin, unable to do what is right in God's eyes.

Unredeemed Body/Flesh: The physical body, along with indwelling sin. This dying body was inherited through the fall of Adam and Eve, in the Garden of Eden. This unredeemed body dictates to the sinful nature of the degenerate man and wins because sadly, sin reigns.

"ONE NEW DUDE"

Divine Nature: The new-self, the new man, is spiritually alive and has power over sin via the Holy Spirit. He is a "Christ-Follower." He is regenerate as God's Holy Spirit has re-generated him. He is set free from sin's former power over him and is now empowered and free to do what is right in God's eyes.

Unredeemed Body/Flesh: The physical body, along with indwelling sin. This dying body was inherited through the fall of Adam and Eve, in the Garden of Eden. This unredeemed body attempts to dictate to the divine nature of the re-generated man but loses because the sin indwelling it no longer reigns. The *One New Dude* reigns through Christ as a partaker of the divine nature.

BEFORE and unless a person is saved, the *old dude* is the inner man. **AFTER** a person is saved, the *One New Dude* is the inner man.

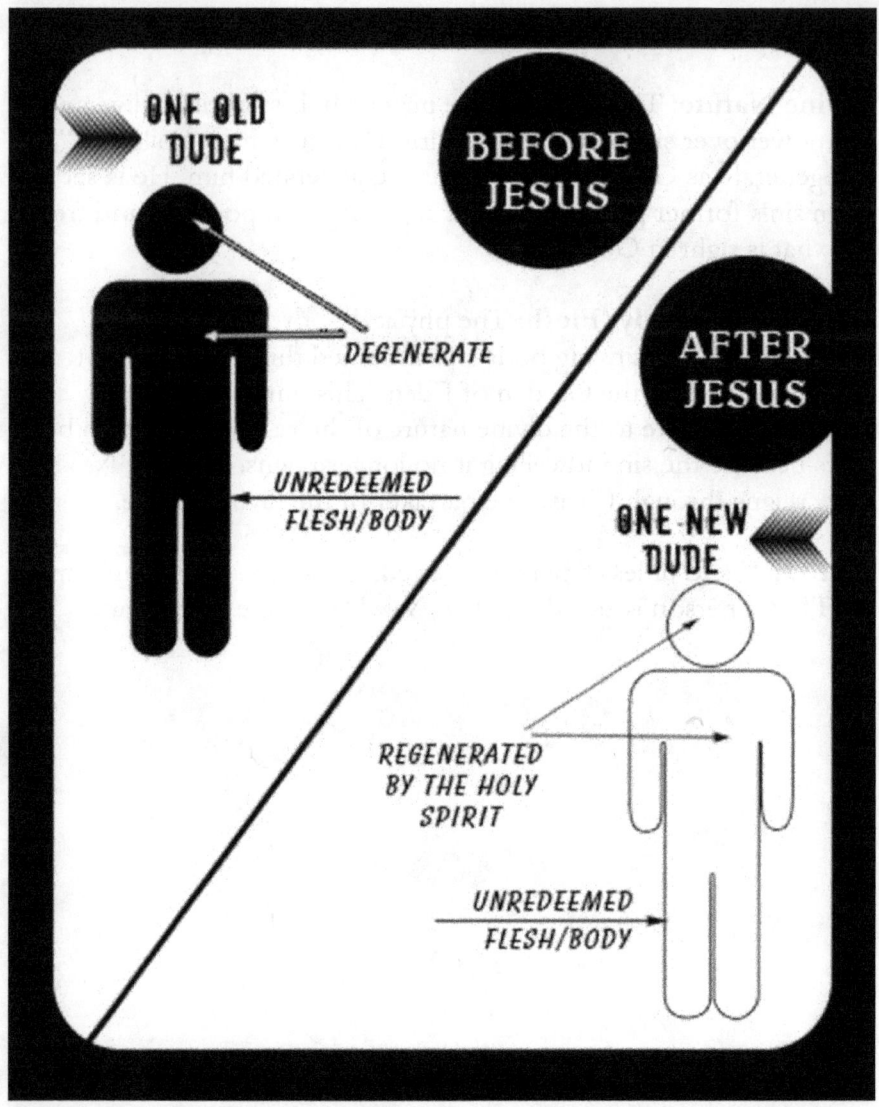

In instances where the old dude isn't put to death by regeneration, sin within the frail, unredeemed body *reigns*. The old man has no power—for he is spiritually dead. The combination of an unredeemed, inner man with an unredeemed body that has indwelling sin is eternally *lethal*.

Spiritually dead men *cannot* and therefore *do not* reign over sin.

On the other hand, when the **old man is dead & buried**—replaced with the new man—the **sin** within the frail body **no longer reigns**. This is because:

1) **The same Spirit who raised Jesus from the dead gives you life.**

   "The Spirit of God, who raised Jesus from the dead, lives in you. And just as God raised Christ Jesus from the dead, he will give life to your mortal bodies by this same Spirit living within you."
   ~ Romans 8:11 NLT

2) **Receiving God's provision for you causes you to reign in life.**

   "For if, by the trespass of the one man, death reigned through that one man, how much more will those who receive God's abundant provision of grace and of the gift of righteousness reign in life through the one man, Jesus Christ."
   ~ Romans 5:17 NIV

   "For sin will have no dominion over you, since you are not under law but under grace."
   ~ Romans 6:14 ESV

   "For one who has died has been set free from sin."
   ~ Romans 6:7 ESV

As *One New Dude*, you have been set free from sin which means you are free from the *power* of sin. Where once sin reigned under the old dude, it no longer reigns because there's *One New Dude* in charge; the same Spirit who raised Christ from the dead. As long as this is *not accepted as truth* the lie blurs your vision of who God says you are.

True humility accepts grace and what God says. False humility may accept some portions of grace, but not all of grace. Partial grace is not true grace. Jesus paid the price for you to have everything He wanted you to have.

For example, if I gave you a million dollars but you only accepted $500k—you rejected what I desired for you to have. I wanted you to have $1 million! This seemed like *too much* for your pride so you *downgraded* my gift by only cashing in on half of it. You just left the other half sitting there collecting dust, never to be used. You rejected an amazing gift because the half you didn't accept or use was *intended to be used for good*. This *good* never happened because it required the remaining $500k.

The old man/sin nature has no power over sin in vessel.

The *flesh/body* that has sin in its members takes *orders* from the *sinful* nature when unredeemed. Those orders are: *"There are no orders! Do whatever you want!"* There is no divine nature present to safely navigate the vessel away from sin.

In the case of divine natured *One New Dude—where* God the Holy Spirit governs the vessel—the *flesh/body* with sin in its members has been in autopilot until the *new Sheriff* arrived. The *deeds* of the *flesh/body* used to be automatic, manifesting consistently. Some say the *deeds of the flesh* are *fallout* from the old self, the sinful nature. This is reasonable, but it could also be the deeds are simply a *result* of the cancer of sin which resides in the *members of the body*—period. This distinction is always worth considering when you consider the *deeds of the flesh*.

So, the difference here is the Holy Spirit is in charge, *not the old man! He's already crucified. Hallelujah!*

By the way, Jesus performed this spiritual circumcision on your behalf so you could be set free and walk as *One New Dude*. His plan was/is not for you to wrestle with what He already defeated. Be set free in the name of Jesus Christ!

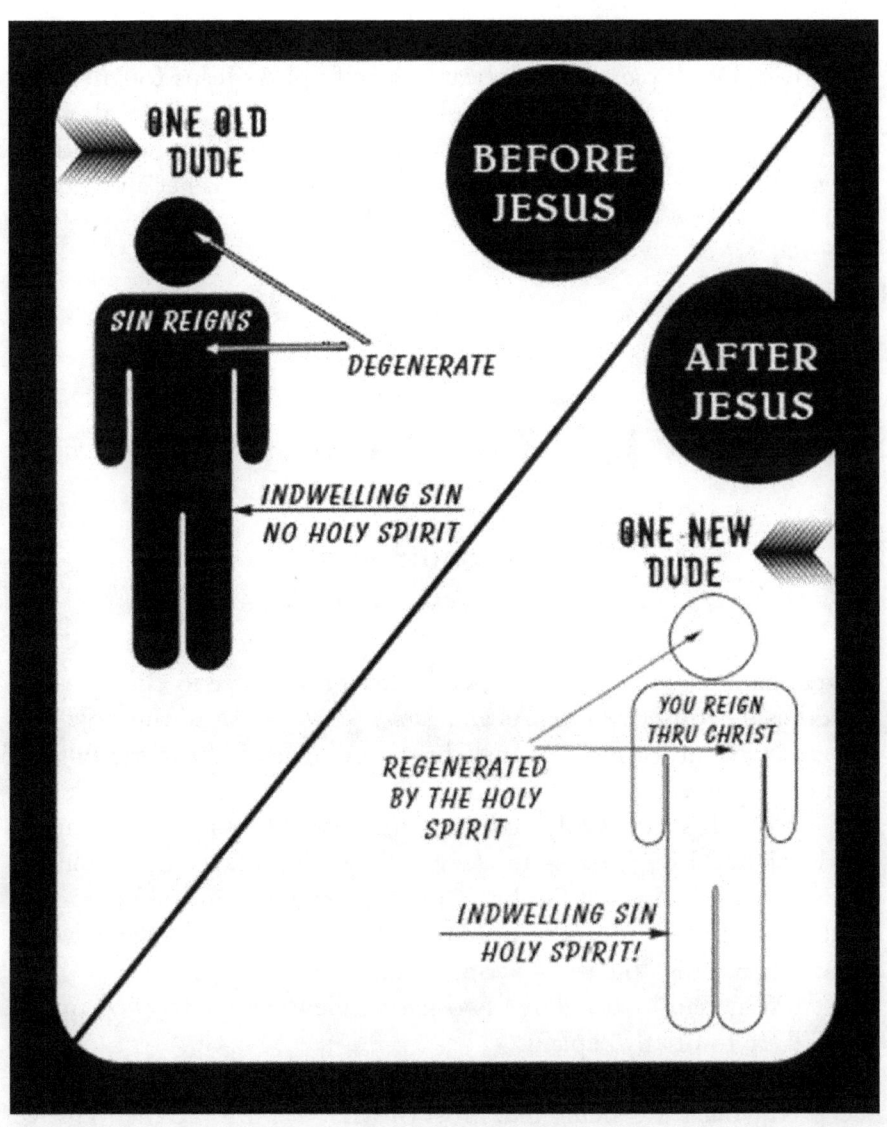

"Then each of you will control his own body and live in holiness and honor—"
~ 1 Thessalonians 4:4

Whenever you may experience your body leaning towards an ungodly behavior or thing don't abandon ship and forget who you are! Even if you fall you have an Advocate. You should never take sin lightly, either. You were purchased at a high price; the precious blood of God the Son!

Still, remember: you live in a body which is yet to be redeemed. Don't panic. Don't beat yourself up! As Jesus fought Satan with God's Word, so shall you wield your *Sword of the Spirit* with what God has told you. Your sin nature was crucified and cut away and you are a new creation in Jesus. Can a brother in Jesus get a witness? *O, What a Savior!*

Come...
Let Us Reason

Responding to Alternate View Advocates

Never changing your mind when it makes good sense to change your mind has its consequences. As an *alternate view advocate* to the *single-nature* viewpoint for most of my Christian journey —I can say this, with confidence—and in faith.

Yes. It's true. Only in the months leading up to the writing of this book had I repented— or *changed my mind*—in favor of the single-natured view. Its impact has been life-changing. If you still hold to a double-natured position there are many good reasons to change your mind. There's also plenty of scripture in support of it.

Why had I trusted in a two-nature view for so long you might ask? I'll try to briefly explain.

Like many who will read this book, I pretty much just accepted what I was being fed. Most of what I *ate* caused me to grow. But then I noticed there was still some *congestion* when it came to my true identity. There's a reasonable possibility, in my opinion, early Study Bible commentators influenced seminary students with their writings while holding to a double-natured viewpoint.

However, are Bible commentator commentaries infallible, as is God's Word? I would suggest, *"No."* What if early reference Bibles were authored by a Christian who held to a single-natured view? Wouldn't most people be fed such an understanding and belief is the appropriate one? I would suggest, *"Yes."*

It's always easier to run with the crowd. I'm not suggesting you *go against the grain—regarding* the sinful nature thing—simply to rebel against what is popular in mainstream Christianity. Not at all. Simply be challenged to test everything as your Bible exhorts. Are you taking the path of least resistance regarding the sinful nature issue? Might I suggest taking the path of *least resistance*, at least in this case, leads to *added resistance* and an unnecessary war within you? Such a path can result in confusion and a *fractured* identity.

When it came to challenging the status quo, demonic spirits appeared to whisper into my spirit: *"Why stand out? Why make any waves? All of these people over here believe Christians must have a sinful nature, plus they have a lot of college degrees so they must be accurate! You'd be foolish to hold a belief contrary to what they are teaching. This walk is hard enough, denying yourself and all this type of thing. Take the path of least resistance; remain in everybody's 'good graces', and just stop pursuing this one-nature-one-identity thing! After all, who are you to tell others what God has done and is saying?"*

As of 2012—and I imagine for quite some time beforehand—there appears to be a popular teaching and attitude surrounding Christians. It saddens me. I hope this book puts a *gigantic, positive dent* into it. My hope is believers will realize the magnitude of God's grace this side of Heaven.

Sometimes *with words* and sometimes *without words* believers inaccurately assess and pass erroneous judgment—when it comes to identity matters. I've had firsthand experience: *"Of course you have two natures. How can you even question this? Are you saying you don't sin? You know you can lose your salvation, don't you!"*

In other words, they seemed to be basically inferring: *"Who is this person with false teaching and thinking he doesn't sin? Quiet down and stop promoting such a thing to believers!"*

By God's grace and in the Spirit of Christ, you do not have to fall into or continue to remain within such a way of thinking—if this is or has been your disposition. As Christians, protecting the truth is important. We're commanded to guard it. Let's not do so at the expense of keeping a brother down, though. We are commanded to build each other up, not clip each other's wings! If a brother is trapped in fear, it's not an excuse to keep a brother back! *Can I get a witness up in here?*

"There is no fear in love, but perfect love casts out fear. For fear has to do with punishment, and whoever fears has not been perfected in love."
~ 1 John 4:18 ESV

Paul Beats Body - Not Old Self

"No, I beat my body and make it my slave so that after I have preached to others, I myself will not be disqualified for the prize."
~ 1 Corinthians 9:27 NIV

If the sin nature was still Paul's *opponent*, why would Paul say he had to beat his body and make it his slave? Paul is the same person who tells us he is *dead*; his old self, his sin nature, is dead. He lives, *yet not he*, but Christ in him lives.

If we do the math we have *one dead old Paul*, one unredeemed body he beats back, who is Spirit-filled, Spirit-empowered, Spirit-led. That's exciting news for you even if it's still sinking in. God is amazing and He thinks you are awesome enough to *substitutionarily* pay your penalty in full—on the Cross—so you could be *One New Dude!*

Recurring Death?

"JZ, Paul indicates he 'dies daily' in 1 Corinthians 15:31. How can you say I don't have to crucify my old man, daily? Paul says it, right there. He 'dies daily!"

"I affirm, brethren, by the boasting in you which I have in Christ Jesus our Lord, <u>I die daily</u>."
~ 1 Corinthians 15: 31-32 NASB

It's an interesting point but only for a moment. Grabbing hold of *scripture snippets* in my new life in Jesus, I had always leaned back onto this verse in order to reconcile—in my mind—why I thought I was called to *"crucify my old man, daily."* I usually just went off memory. Since those words jumped out at me, I held onto this little phrase.

Wrestling with and trying to understand what was going on inside of me, it seemed inevitable a preacher would mention *the old man*. It was and is as if they are continually re-affirming an ugly sin nature still alive within the believer. These three words above would trigger the thought, *"I am at war within myself! There's two of me!"* There certainly is some warfare going on and Jesus certainly wins, but it isn't with your *old man*. He's dead. Jesus already dealt with that dude.

OK, so let's try to add some context to this next one and work through it. It should be brief.

"Why are we also in danger every hour? I affirm, brethren, by the boasting in you which I have in Christ Jesus our Lord, I die daily. If from human motives I fought with wild beasts at Ephesus, what does it profit me?"
~ 1 Corinthians 15:31 NASB

Paul is not discussing any type of crucifixion. God isn't addressing anything regarding you putting to death some alter-ego or sinful nature that resides in you. Why? It's because it isn't there to *shadow box or contend with you* every day. Your body needs to be kept in check but the *crucified* sinful nature is a defeated foe.

Let's jump over to another translation…

"For I swear, dear brothers and sisters, that I face death daily. This is as certain as my pride in what Christ Jesus our Lord has done in you."
~ 1 Corinthians 15: 31-32 NLT

Let's add even more context; a verse before and a verse after. *"Context"* without *"text"* leaves you with what? That's correct…a *"con!"*

"And why should we ourselves risk our lives hour by hour? For I swear, dear brothers and sisters, that I face death daily. This is as certain as my pride in what Christ Jesus our Lord has done in you. And what value was there in fighting wild beasts—those people of Ephesus—if there will be no resurrection from the dead? And if there is no resurrection, 'Let's feast and drink, for tomorrow we die!'"
~ 1 Cor. 15: 31-32 NLT

Paul doesn't *"crucify his old self, daily."* Denying yourself to follow

Jesus—while once more may *seem* like a slow death or *dying daily* at times—it is not. You can't die if you're already dead. Paul and you and I ... as Christians, are already dead according to God. Those who belong to Christ *have crucified the flesh.* You live, *yet not you,* but Christ in you lives. Whether or not we trust what God says is another story. Thinking incorrectly about a specific matter has never been a good excuse to continue on thinking incorrectly, right?

Paul faced death—daily. This is all he's saying. When you take this verse the way God intended through Paul, you are left without a verse which supports the idea the sinful nature is still alive and needs to be put to death. Jesus did this already at the cross. You stepped into this gift when you accepted Christ.

This verse is even further established in Romans 8:

> *As it is written: "For your sake we face death all day long; we are considered as sheep to be slaughtered."*
> **~ Romans 8:36 NIV**

Crucifixion is an event as baptism is an event. Otherwise, baptism would be a drowning, isn't that right?[39]

Also, see Galatians 5:24. These are all *key-turning* verses. Contrary to the way many popular teachings are conveyed, crucifixion is *not* sanctification. See Romans 6:6 and Colossians 2:11. If something is dead it can't be alive. This must be settled in the mind once and for all if you are to walk as *One New Dude*.

Dirty Deeds

"JZ, I 'feel' God gets more glory when He's put into a battle with the 'old man', my 'sin nature' and they 'duke it out', then God wins. I like how this sounds. That's my feeling and I'm sticking to it!"

> *"For if you live by its dictates, you will die. But if through the power of the Spirit you put to death the deeds of your sinful nature, you will live."*
> **~ Romans 8:13 NLT**

Why did God through Paul, instruct us to *"put to death the <u>deeds</u> of your sinful nature,"* through Christ's Spirit, rather than to *"put to death your <u>sinful nature</u>?"* The Creator of the universe isn't a man He should lie, right?[40] Nor, is He a man He should contradict Himself. *The old self* or *sin nature* is off limits. Your old self—your sin nature—occupies this bucket. It's a bucket *for and of...* the deceased.

Some might have conveniently, albeit inaccurately, reasoned out it makes good sense to them to keep a crucified sin nature *alive*— at least enough for it to be recognized as fighting against the indwelling Holy Spirit, daily. Then, God *gets more glory* because He is victorious by ultimately *putting to death* the sinful nature.

But Dude, as we have seen, Jesus has *already taken care of the sin nature*. You must receive this grace if you are to walk as *One New Dude*. Contrary to the above reasoning, God *does not "get more glory"* when we *don't* accept pure grace.

Pride and fleshy works point us *away* from Jesus and instead point us to *ourselves*, right? A good case could be made God does get *all* of the intended glory in the single-nature/single-identity view. He doesn't choose to resurrect what's already been crucified, and He doesn't need to *battle with* what He's already defeated and instructed the new creation to *"throw off."*

Jesus gets credit for the spiritual circumcision performed at the cross He would otherwise *not* properly get credit for. Equally is his Spirit putting to death the *deeds* of either what the crucified man left behind or what the unredeemed body would otherwise naturally manifest. When we split things out properly God is getting all of the glory to be sure!

"For if you live by <u>its dictates</u>, you will die. But if through the power of the Spirit you put to death the deeds of your sinful nature, you will live."
~ Romans 8:13 NLT

"its dictates" - What is *"its?"* Is it unreasonable to hear and reason out what is being said here? Referring to the *flesh* need not require *flesh* be synonymous with the *sinful nature*—at least in this instance. It can easily be concluded God is informing us we have *flesh*, an *unredeemed body* which, apart from the presence of God the Holy Spirit, will *"dictate."*

It reminds me of an analogy. A dog is left to itself, not

dominated or *ruled* over by its Master. This dog will oftentimes—by default—*dominate* or *rule* the house and its owner!

It's not a perfectly harmonious analogy, but it should serve to get the point across. In other words, the dog is not an apples-to-apples comparison with the human body. Avoid reading into things any deeper than what is intended on this one.

The point is simply this: The *physical body* is going to *drive* if the *new man* doesn't drive. That's how it is with the *old dude*. There should be no question however, *Who* is in charge with the *One New Dude*. The more you abide in Christ and the Word, the less confusion you will have regarding what God says. Faith in Christ is communion with God. To lack faith, on the other hand, could cause some problems. Sanctification is God's plan. You get to participate *through faith*. Let God renew your mind with eternal truth!

The old man is dead and buried but the body is not. The *flesh* or *body* no longer rules or reigns because the *old man is dead* and sin is not your master. You are under grace as a blood-bought Dude! The new man—alive in Christ—*rules and reigns through Christ*. It's all about Jesus and He chose your house to make his home. Get used to it and know who you are!

By the way, this is precisely why the *unregenerate* man is a slave to sin. That dude has no power over sin. The *One New Dude*, however, does have this power in Christ.

In This Corner!

The Spirit and the flesh are opposed to one another; true. Yet, this does not require *"flesh"* to have or be a nature of its own. Cannot the Spirit choose his own battles? Cannot the Spirit decide the *flesh*, which is the *old man/sinful nature*, be crucified at the cross with Jesus, as He has?

Then, the *flesh* which includes the physical body, and the *deeds of the flesh*—which are what remains from the crucified flesh/sin nature—is lined up for the final stage of the battle? Together, redeemed soul and the Holy Spirit put to death those deeds!

When *your* efforts get more into the spotlight than *Christ's* finished work *(as can become the case when sinful natures which are revealed to be crucified are still getting recognition as if they are alive and active)*, grace tends to get pushed to the backseat, doesn't it? Works can rear their ugly head. It's at least possible, isn't it?

When I used to think I had a sinful nature (as I was taught) as a born-again believer, my understanding of what Christ accomplished was blurred. I wasn't even aware of all He had done. Once I *sought, asked, and knocked...* I discovered what Christ had done. I had to either accept it (stop doing the work of *"crucifying my sinful nature"*) or reject it by continuing with this so called *daily crucifixion*. It had to be one or the other. One was grace; the other was works because it rejected pure grace.

It was then the following verse jumped out at me. Even though it contrasts the works-oriented, religious individual with a person of faith and recipient of grace, you might be able to see how *working* can creep in and severely tamper with the foundation of *righteousness*:

> *"And to the one who <u>does not work but believes</u> in him who justifies the ungodly, his faith is counted as righteousness,"*
> **~ Romans 4:5 ESV**

If a believer is truly resting in Jesus and not working, then why does so much attention get taken away from Jesus and put onto the forgiven sinner's efforts? If Christ has crucified my sinful nature—if it's been buried in baptism and cut away by Christ's already accomplished spiritual circumcision at the cross—why in the world would I or any believer be spending any time *whatsoever* fighting this deceased thing? Especially if I've been obedient to *throw this old thing off* as I've been commanded? Does it not rob Jesus of what is due Him with respect to his finished work? He is to be worshiped! *Hallelujah!*

Are you *more inclined* to worship Jesus having learned He has set you free from your old self and sinful nature, or are you *less inclined*? If you don't think He did it—the way He intended for it to be understood & embraced—and don't worship Him in the way you otherwise would, grace is cheapened; is it not? Is the joyful heart the same joyful heart it would be if this eternal truth of Christ's finished work is not realized?

This is not a small thing! Can we get an *"Amen!"* up in here? Shout to the Lord! He is amazing!

This is great news for believers and unbelievers, alike! Once you are sealed with the Holy Spirit, the victory is yours because Jesus doesn't and didn't lose! The Spirit of Christ is cleaning house! You have been redeemed! You have power! You have authority and it's all because of the blood of Jesus. All because Jesus lives in you!

In stage one *(let's call it stage one)*... Jesus nailed it to the cross! Your sin nature done away with! Your *old self* done away with! You didn't know it was going down, but Jesus was handling some business on your behalf. Stage two is house-cleaning.

A few more thoughts regarding your situation: Your unredeemed physical body is a temporary tent. The flesh or physical body can have and does have its own appetites. This is all without the need for the *nature in charge* to have those same appetites.

Once examined carefully, it's clear God *splits out* the nature from the body. Nature relates to your spirit-man. By this I'm suggesting you, as a forgiven sinner, are *new* and a *partaker of the divine nature*. You still have a physical body which has its own appetites—some of which may be contrary to your nature. This is why God is *going to redeem your physical body*. You need a new one, if you hadn't noticed. This body is not built to last forever!

As a Christ-follower, your current body is no longer governed by an unregenerate man. God has positioned things, as such. It is now ruled over by a regenerated person, one who is a partaker of the divine nature and filled with God's Spirit. This is you, *One New Dude!* The new body is coming for you, as a believer. *Hallelujah!* Jesus has a new body waiting for you! Are you ready to get into this thing, or what? *Praise God for his amazing grace!*

Kaboom!

Deeds of the flesh will manifest in one's life, when either: *a.)* they are not regenerated by the Holy Spirit, or *b.)* when they don't know their identity, in Christ. For the true Christ-follower, they are the very things over which the old, sinful nature had no power. They are *fallout* or *vestiges* of the sinful nature, which is now and already—crucified.

> *"Now the deeds of the flesh are evident, which are: immorality, impurity, sensuality, idolatry, sorcery, enmities, strife, jealousy, outbursts of anger, disputes, dissensions, factions, envying, drunkenness, carousing, and things like these, of which I forewarn you, just as I have forewarned you, that those who practice such things will not inherit the kingdom of God."*
> **~ Galatians 5:19-21**

Please consider the following: If the cancer of sin dwells in the members of the body as we have learned, then are the *deeds of the flesh* restricted to only being associated with the sinful nature, which is now crucified? *"Flesh"* can refer to *human* or *sinful* nature, but we know it can also be translated and referred to as the *physical body*.

Is there any room for the possibility the *deeds of the flesh* are simply the very deeds the *physical body* leans towards, apart from God? Aren't these *deeds*—which are associated with the sinful nature and unregenerate sinner—finding their origin in a fallen, unredeemed physical body? I would suggest, yes.

While this is another example of an analogy which may ultimately fall short, it can still serve as a helpful word-picture as you press on into your journey.

Let's say a *major* war occurred. Huge bombs were dropped from above, programmed to seek out and obliterate targets of interest. You then walked amongst the areas of land which were bombarded. The highest target of interest—The *Main Control Center* of the enemy, where all of the evil direction was given—was taken out with astonishing precision.

However, during your walk you also came across some radios and some electronic gear which were previously attached to the main control center. These items, having been cut off from the main computer of the Main Control Center, no longer had the impact they once possessed. In fact, their chance of survival was not looking good! They were always dependent upon the Main Control Center but that was obliterated!

As the final phase of the war plan, RF energy and electronics-detecting robots are sent out. On the ground, they seek out and destroy any remaining radios and electronics gear. It renders the enemy completely defeated, making the mission an undeniable and thorough success!

In a similar way, the bombing of the Main Control Center would be akin to what Jesus did to your *flesh* when referring to the old man/sinful nature. Jesus had a specific objective regarding your sinful nature. It was to target it, seek it out and take it out! You could say Christ was on a mission and He accomplished the mission. He cried out from the cross, *"Tetelestai!"* or *"It is finished!"* Mission accomplished! Praise his mighty name! Feel free to say, "Jesus, thank You!"

The deeds of the crucified sin nature are akin to the radios and electronic gear. They may flicker but with very little hope of survival. In fact, their hope for survival becomes increasingly dire as God the Holy Spirit is now *on the ground*, seeking out and destroying those deeds of the flesh. *Hallelujah!* The Lord is undeniably thorough! He who began a good work in you will continue it until the day of Christ Jesus! Can a *One New Dude* get a witness up in here!

"So put to death <u>the sinful, earthly things lurking within</u> you. Have nothing to do with sexual immorality, impurity, lust, and evil desires. Don't be greedy, for a greedy person is an idolater, worshiping the things of this world."
~ Colossians 3:5

Watch now. Same verse, different way of translating, same general idea, though:

Therefore <u>consider the members of your earthly body as dead</u> to immorality, impurity, passion, evil desire, and greed, which amounts to idolatry.
~ Colossians 3:5 NASB

The above verse lines up just fine with the below verse. Both verses speak about *sinful things*, or a *sin principle*, which lurks in the believer. It's consistent with sanctification and *requires not* a *sinful nature*, based upon the text. It's consistent with sanctification because you are having your mind renewed by God's truth, through his Word. The Lord is telling you *what went down* at the cross and *what went down* when you received Christ. He's revealing to you *who you are, what you are, with what you are left, and what is coming.* So, let's get back to the verses:

> *"but I see <u>in my members</u> another law waging war against the law of my mind and making me captive to <u>the law of sin that dwells in my members.</u>"*
> **~ Romans 7:23**

Important to note the term *"members"* is identified as to the "location" where *"sin"* finds it's *"base of operation."* This is the *body's* members. In choosing a side on this one, you are able to make a distinction between your body and your identity. You'll either *fight with or somehow carry around a personality that is no longer you*—the old self, the sin nature/old man—who we have learned from God is already dead. Or…you *will not carry that person around,* you *will not believe such a nature or identity exists any longer,* and *you will walk in true newness of life.*

One idea of *newness* dukes it out with a sin nature scripture states to be *crucified,* the other *newness* gets into agreement with God and trusts. *"Yes Father, Jesus took this person away and I accept payment in full!"*

Full and pure grace. Not partial grace. Partial grace cheapens grace and adds to it with self-effort. Cooperate with God in your sanctification, but please do not do so at the expense of grace. Grace *misunderstood* is not grace *realized.* God pointed this out through Paul when Jews were trying to add circumcision to grace in Galatians.

Let's look once more by going back to these recent texts, shall we?

God could have used Paul to say, *"In my old man"* or *"in my sinful nature"* dwells my sin, couldn't He have? However, God chose to make a distinction and instead used *"members"* of the body, or *parts of the physical body.* This more closely describes Paul's *outer man,* not his *inner man.* Paul is speaking as a redeemed and blood-bought new creation, a partaker of the divine nature. He observes and makes note of this *sin principle* at work, within his *body parts.*

Finally, if sin didn't *cling to our flesh*…if sin didn't cling to your *physical body,* it would seem unlikely a redeemed body would need to be part of God's redemption package. As it is, God has promised more to come following his down-payment of sealing you with his Holy Spirit. This came at the moment you received Christ. This promise is a redeemed body.

"For we know that the whole creation groans and suffers the pains of childbirth together until now. And not only this, but also we ourselves, having the first fruits of the Spirit, even we ourselves groan within ourselves, waiting eagerly for our adoption as sons, the redemption of our body."
~ **Romans 8:22-23 NASB**

Sanctification Insights

Based upon the presupposition you are *body, soul and spirit* and since we are discussing sanctification, why don't we do this?

What I'd like to do is offer to you some encouraging insight. You might be getting discouraged or confused as God conforms and aligns your thinking with His eternal truth. Know and remember: Jesus accomplished what was required for you to be *One New Dude* with no *other dude* in the picture.

This said, if you've been a Christian for a while you might still be white-knuckling things a bit in order to hold onto a theology with which you have grown comfortable. That's OK! There is no condemnation for those in Christ Jesus![41] Old habits seem to die hard. They can also change in a moment with a change of mind! If it's you I'm describing, just consider God's desire for you. I believe it is to *discover* and *be established* in your singular, divine nature.

When God looks at you He sees Jesus—not your shortcomings. If you received Jesus by grace through faith, why would you want to focus primarily on your performance as you proceed? It wouldn't make sense. Focus on Jesus and constantly affirm your faith only in Him. Once you are born-again, getting caught up in your performance and feeling condemned over your every thought shifts the focus from Jesus to you. Conversely, maintaining a steady focus upon Jesus with continual awareness He lives in you, bears fruit which would otherwise not be realized.

As we discuss sanctification, let's revisit a few terms. With these terms are a few clarifying bullet points. The definitions are not set in stone, but they should be reasonable enough for our purposes.

Humanness or *flesh*
- Body
- Mind
- Emotions

Soul
- *Mind* - **old:** not set on the Spirit / **new:** set on the Spirit
- *Will* - **old:** "*my will*" / **new:** "*Thy will*"
- *Emotions* - **old:** negatively impacted by sinful behavior and thinking. Depression, confusion, etc. / **new:** positively impacted by Spirit and Word. Joy, peace, etc.

Consider this:
- Jesus indicated God's Word sanctifies you, makes you clean.
- God planned you would be washed by the water of the Word.[42]
- Psalms states God's law/Word converts/revives the soul.

Here's the point: Once Jesus saves you and makes you *One New Dude*, you have only begun to have your soul washed clean from the grit and grime of your former way of life. It's akin to *shampooing your mind* with God's eternal truth regarding who you really are. Knowing who you are directly impacts how you think and act.

For example, if a person is a man and *thinks* he is a woman, this is going to have a direct impact on his lifestyle, including what he says and how he behaves. In a similar way, if you think you are a new creation in Christ who still has a sinful nature, then it's hard to believe *how you act, how you think* or *what your view of God is* will *not* be impacted. On the other hand, if you think your sinful nature has been crucified because God says it has, then how you view God and how you act is directly impacted by this, as well.

Furthermore, you need to hold your ground. Satan wants you to panic! Jesus said he is a liar and the father of lies; a murderer.[43] He wants you to go down. He'll even whisper *suicide* to you. Your enemy is not pulling any punches.

Is it God's will you beat yourself down and you have your true identity as a *sinner*? Is this why he re-created you? *"Hey everyone, I'm a sinner! Jesus saved me...I'm a sinner and always will be!"*

OK, OK... we get it. You are a *saint* now, though! A *son* of the Most High. This is who you are. Can you walk in this without feeling guilty about it? Oh, others will try to make you feel guilty, but what about God? Is the Holy Spirit the One tearing you down rather than building you up? Did Jesus die so you could feel guilty claiming promises which come from Him?

Your identity is *a son; a saint*. A *partaker of the divine nature*. Jesus is alive in you. No longer you, but Jesus. Was Jesus a sinner? Of course not. The Holy Spirit who raised Jesus from the dead who lives in *you* now. A sinner? The Holy Spirit?

You are hidden in Christ. Jesus didn't save you so your identity would be: *"Sinner!"* C'mon now. True humility accepts grace. Identifying yourself *(if you are indeed saved)* as a sinner rather than a saint or a son—is this really why Christ paid such a high price? *"Sinners reign in life!"*...that's the message?

A sinner practices sin. Do you practice sin or righteousness? By faith in Christ, you are righteous. Do you have faith in Christ? Satan tells you you're good-for-nothing. God says you are a son, back in relationship. Claim your sonship!

So then, again—what about all the junk still trying to come up on you? You wanna know what it is? Welcome to spiritual warfare! We're not going to explore it right now. Just consider this though, if you would. It all blends in together:

While you are being sanctified and coming into conformity with God's truth, your soul is being converted. You were transformed and are being transformed. You were saved and are being saved. Your mind is new and is being renewed.

Try to imagine this. Picture God's truth pouring over the top of you, working its way from your head to your toes. Sort of like you're taking a shower. God's Word is cleansing and renewing you. You have new thoughts and desires then an old thought pops into your head. Perhaps it's an old way of thinking. But you are new. You received God's grace and empowerment in Christ, already.

Warfare 101 is you handle it like this:

"'We are destroying speculations and every lofty thing raised up against the knowledge of God, and we are taking every thought captive to the obedience of Christ,"
~ 2 Corinthians 10:5 NASB

How does this play into my having one nature—not two—you might ask?

Here's how. Just because you are under construction, so to speak, does not require there be any place at all for what's already been *cut away, crucified and buried*.

Any vestiges that might surface of the old you are only that; *vestiges*. God is at work in you. You are working out your salvation. Your mind is being renewed. God is in control, not the *old you*. God is not fighting the *old you*; this battle's over and Jesus was the Victor. *Scoreboard!*

Don't feel so obligated to hold to a view which states you have a sinful nature. Remnants of the old which have been replaced with the new do not warrant *nature status*. Is God telling you after the cross you are stuck with and have to do battle with your old self? Or, does He tell you this: it's all over for the old self, it's crucified. So get rid of it! *Throw it off!*

It's like a monkey on your back if you don't obey God, isn't it? I used to think I had to carry that thing around, and fight it while I carried it. *Throw that thing off! Right believing leads to right living!*

Becoming You - Sanctification

If you are blowing the whistle on me you can stop. I fully agree. *Everything is OK! Sanctification is* the process of becoming more *like Jesus*, to be *conformed into the image of God's Son*.[44] Yes! You are correct! If the above section title captured your *"test all things"* attention, then good work. You have passed this test and *should* test all things, by all means!

Yet also, know this: this whole sanctification thing started when God supernaturally transformed you into *One New Dude…* Dude! When you are *sanctified* you are set apart unto God. It's the same word for holiness in the Greek.

As a Christian, you are likely familiar with sanctification. Let's still take a brief look at its meaning, since we'll be relating it to your identity. There is what I'll refer to as three *types* of sanctification[45] represented in God's Word:

1. **Immediate** - *When you were saved, you were set apart for God.*
2. **Progressive** - *Experiencing being set apart via the continual obedience to God's Word.*
3. **Ultimate** - *Perfected into Christ's likeness. God has already perfected you, in a sense, if you are in Jesus.[46] You are simply awaiting the full realization of it!*

It would be a good thing to know who you are *right now*, while still on your way to glory, wouldn't it? Let me say it again. When you trusted Christ to save you, *God transformed you into One New Dude!*

> *"Therefore, if anyone is in Christ, he is a new creation; the old has gone, the new has come!"*
> **~ 2 Corinthians 5:17**

That's you, Dude! The critical thing to come to grips with, though... is: Are you going to accept *being* the actual *One New Dude* God has made you to be? The *One New Dude* God made you to be *shares no space* with a crucified old dude.

Becoming you does not necessitate you *are not already you*. This might sound like a contradiction, but it would not necessarily be the case—that is, if God's objective for the new creation is taken into consideration. If *becoming you* involves actually trusting and believing what God says regarding your identity, then it would not be a contradiction so far as I can see. This is because in order to *become you*, you must embrace by faith what God says *about you*.

What if God says something which is true about you, but you don't believe it? What if you say you believe it, but are not fully persuaded in your mind? Does God's truth regarding who you are, in reality, change? Of course not.

Let's not overlook this, either. This is not a small matter. Just because a person gets saved by receiving Jesus and being born from above does not mean their faith is rock-solid and everything God says they trust as true. Once more, they may concede God doesn't lie and therefore, what He says must be true. Yet, isn't it possible for a person to do this but still have serious doubts and faith issues regarding something specific God says, if they were to dig a bit deeper?

This should sound reasonable. We are all faced with faith challenges to help us to grow. Nonetheless, this does not mean just because one new creation *gets it* on a certain date and passes *Go!* all others do likewise. To believe all *believers* trust at the same time with the same measure of faith doesn't ring accurate or biblical. *So, what am I getting at?*

If God tells you the truth about yourself—and you fully accept it even when it's hard to believe—then you are rewarded however God chooses to reward you. Maybe it's an accelerated path to closer relationship with Him? Deep gratitude tends to go further than discontentment, doesn't it? Perhaps it's a deeper level of peace, or maybe even financial blessing. Everything is on the table with the Lord. God is a *Rewarder* of those who diligently seek Him, right? We also know it's impossible to please God without faith.

Keep in mind, your level of faith in what God says about a specific verse may differ from another's level of faith in what God says in the same verse. What if another professing Christian doesn't believe the verse *in the same way* you believe the verse? Maybe they conclude it means something other than what you believe it means?

Yet, hypothetically and to make the point, what if God actually desires for each of his children to accept the verse exactly as He stated it in the text because it is his eternal plan to bless each by receiving in faith what He is saying?

Would you then conclude God would attribute an exercising of faith to *both* individuals? More specifically, since only God knows hearts and judges flawlessly, isn't it possible only one of the two *believers* accept God at his Word and benefit from it, at least in that moment? If not, then it would seem you can either *take* or *not take* God at his Word and still be rewarded the same. This doesn't sound biblical, does it?

Now that hard lines have been drawn to illustrate a point, let's relax those hard lines. In the Spirit of Christ, dwelling in God's amazing grace, let's concede God's truth unfolding within each of our lives is usually at a varying pace and concentration. Wounded souls, for example, might have a hard time forgiving themselves or believing *anything* good about themselves. Throw in grace and the inheritance for those in Christ and things may even become a bit overwhelming to them.

Even though you are saved when you received Christ, you were and are still left to rely upon God the Holy Spirit. You are to work out your salvation under God's power.

God the Holy Spirit indwells you. *Fact!* Remember when you invited Him in?

> *"But you did not learn Christ in this way, if indeed you have heard Him and have been taught in Him, just as truth is in Jesus, that, in reference to your former manner of life, you lay aside the old self, which is being corrupted in accordance with the lusts of deceit, and that you be renewed in the spirit of your mind, and put on the new self, which in the likeness of God has been created in righteousness and holiness of the truth."*
> **~ Ephesians 4:20-24 NASB**

YOU ARE NEW. Getting your body, mind and emotions on board with what God has done for you and told you He has done requires both grace & faith. By grace you have been saved, through faith; right? Living apart from God and truth for years at a time certainly comes with its own consequences. By this I mean, it's quite normal to become very aware of those things within you and those things around you which are not holy or pleasing to God. But you know what? God's bigger! *Hallelujah!*

It's also still reasonable to conclude you are left with *humanness* after becoming *One New Dude*. What you are left with is not your *old self*, or what is commonly referred to as a *sinful nature*. What has already been crucified cannot be alive. That sinful nature God tells you *is crucified*. You also *buried* it at baptism, *after* you changed your mind and realized Christ saved you.

In addition to what it's already been defined as above, parts of your humanness are progressively coming into conformity with what God says you are: *a saint; a son.* A person who seeks after Him, who desires to obey Him, rather than one who automatically disobeys Him. As *One New Dude*, even if you disobey it's an exception— not the rule. This is not how it was with the old you, which proves you are new! Your current desire is to be obedient to God. It's not just in lip service, but it's in actual lifestyle change. Unlike the sinner, you know God is good and has your best in mind.

Nevertheless, as a young baby picks up harmful things within reach only to put them into their mouth, so is the *One New Dude* who has yet to realize proper nutrition. Instead of craving the pure milk of God's Word, and instead of thinking accurately regarding identity, the *One New Dude* undergoes an *identity discovery process*. God has revealed who he now is, but each dude must come to trust what God says, individually.

Just as the baby hasn't come to a full realization they are a human being, so the *One New Dude* also finds himself in a similar identity discovery process. The baby's actions aren't always consistent with a human being. Swallowing plastic isn't consistent with reasonable human beings, is it? Something just isn't *clicking* in there. At some point, they grow in understanding and stop thinking plastic is the appropriate way of nutrition.

Similarly, the *One New Dude's* actions aren't always consistent with who they are—a partaker of the divine nature. God, being your heavenly Father, is training you up as his child. This is why you need his Word daily. With it come loving commands and exhortations which pour truth into your life and being. Scripture, such as the verses below, demonstrate even as *One New Dude* you are being taught and reminded of who you truly are. God's plan is for you to act and think consistently with it, not contrarily:

> *"Do not lie to one another, seeing that you have put off the old self with its practices and <u>have put on the new self, which is being renewed in knowledge after the image of its creator.</u>"*
> **~ Colossians 3: 9-10**

Romans 7

Whether or not Romans 7 is a description of an unsaved dude, a saved dude, or both—scholars continue the debate. It's probably a snapshot of both. That said, a struggle is clearly presented.

For those who believe Romans 7 is not describing a Christian, there is nothing to discuss regarding sanctification. Only a *believer* is sanctified and goes through progressive sanctification. However, some do believe *all of* or at least the *second half* of Romans 7 describes a born-again believer. In both of these viewpoints there definitely is a believer struggling. We hear it firsthand from Paul.

Nevertheless, since God has used Paul to reveal the very real state of the sinful nature for the believer which is *crucified, dead, and buried*... there's no reason why you shouldn't be able to consider what is being proposed:

Sanctification, I would propose, is an *umbrella* under which the believer *is becoming* what God says he has become, at least in one sense. That is *One New Dude*. A new creation! Paul indicated as a Christian he was a new creation. He also indicated he was *still pressing forward* towards perfection. Part of this *pressing forward* might include some time to *sync up* with God's truth.

Just because Paul humbly expresses his shortcomings does not negate everything else he has already said in Romans 6, and will say afterward in Romans 8. Paul was human just like you and me. Paul was being transformed as he daily recognized God had already transformed him. You can take immense comfort in knowing even the great apostle Paul recognized himself as one new creation, even in the midst of his struggles. Paul indicated more than once it was no longer the old Paul who lived.

You are lovingly commanded by your loving Creator to *"be being filled with the Holy Spirit."* God, the Holy Spirit, is happy to empower you in replacing your old self with *One New Dude*. He is happy to use you as a vessel of honor for His unique purposes. *Hallelujah!* What a privilege! Jesus chose you! You must be amazing for Jesus to die *for* you—then come to make his home *with* you—leading you home to the Promised Land!

Jesus answered him, "If anyone loves me, he will keep my word, and my Father will love him, and we will come to him and make our home with him."
~ **John 14:23 ESV**

The Scanning

It's time for another word picture. Consider the document scanner. You may even own one. Today, they are often incorporated into your multi-functional printers. A document scanner scans a hard-copy document such as a photo or letter-sized document, then creates a digital version to be placed on your hard drive.

Now, consider this. The *old man* or *sinful nature* doesn't have spiritual life. There is no presence of God the Holy Spirit, nor is there any proclivity to continually be in the Bible. The result is no *scan* or *sanctification* occurs. There is no *sealing* of the Holy Spirit on that lost soul. This is paramount. The more you grasp this the less you will succumb to the identity lie you are not *One New Dude!* Oftentimes, we can think, *"I have these horrible thoughts and revenge in my heart… therefore, I must not be new and I must be the same old person!"*

Yet, the more you trust what God says the less you will trust the lie of the enemy. This holds true especially if/when you feel embarrassed or confused *(or both)* you thought or acted contrary to your divine nature and God's will. This is faith in action! You are always exercising faith. The question is, is your faith staying on target with what God says, or is it being misdirected to the enemy? Many people say they believe, but believe what and who? Let's narrow it down further to Christians. Many say they trust God's Word, but isn't it possible to *not always* trust what God says?

If we're all candid about it, of course it's possible! Our faith is still growing, to be sure. This conceded, let's make sure we're grabbing hold of and prioritizing this true identity stuff before running onto the next thing. Equally important would be recognizing that although new, you are still a work in progress. There's nothing meriting a state of panic just because you don't *feel* a certain way. Faith in Christ isn't a feeling, as you may already well know. Well then? Faith isn't a feeling when it comes to identity, either. You will be amazed if you get into the habit of just responding to any situation with something like this:

"OK…this terrible thing happened. This thing threw me or that thing shook me. These things may be, yet it doesn't change anything. I'm a new creation in Christ. Greater is He who is in me. I'm still new. I'm still forgiven! I'm still more than a conqueror! Not because of anything I've done. It's all about Jesus and I'm a son! He chose me! If God is for me and is in me, who or what can defeat me? OK, so I'm not perfect, but…I reach towards it! Let me tell you how good God is! Did you know He so loved you He sent Jesus to die on a cross so you could be with Him, both now and forever?"

As you are washed in this word picture—*scanned* by God's Word—make sure you are continually wielding your sword against the lies of the enemy. If Jesus used the sword to defeat Satan's lies, how much more shall you as Satan and others call into question your true identity in Jesus? Don't forget Job's counselors. Even believers can draw the wrong conclusions. Instead of building you up, they tear you down. Choose to focus *not upon your shortcomings* as God changes you, but rather upon the grace He has given by adopting you as his son.

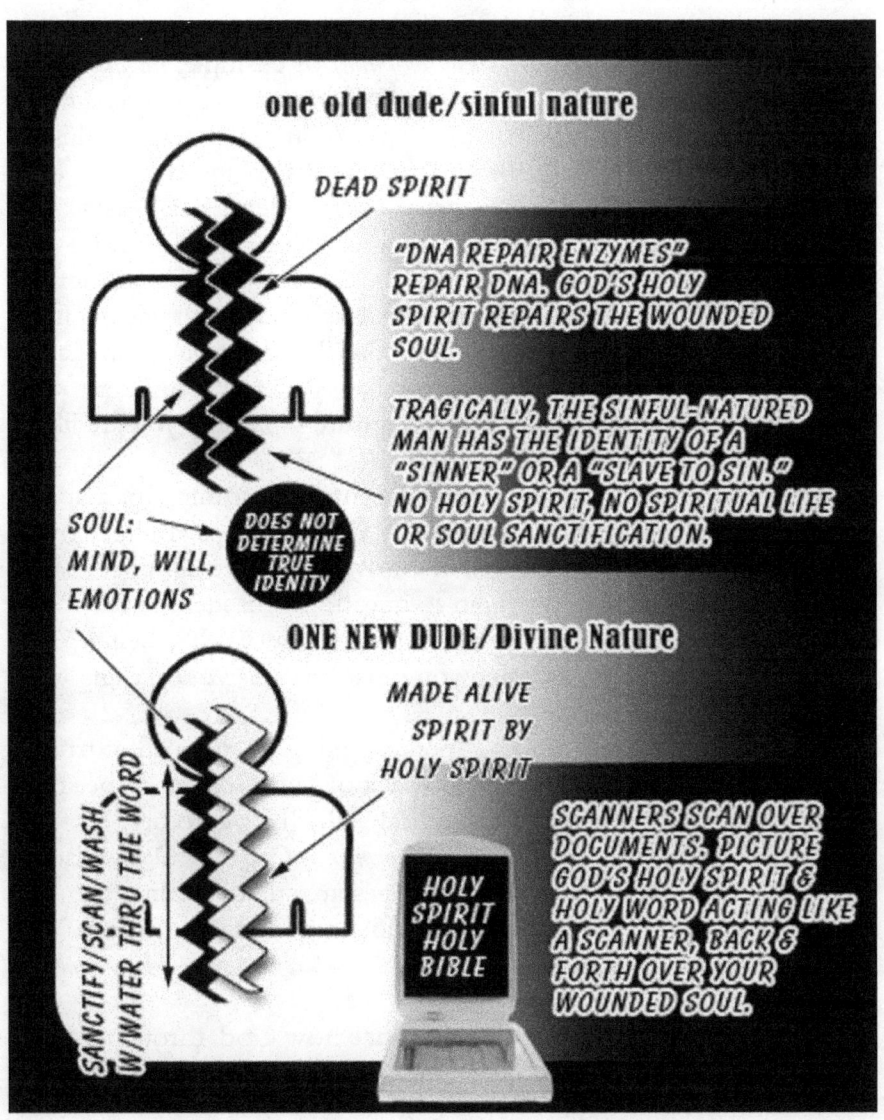

Poof!

To recognize *transformation* can occur progressively would not preclude it from also occurring immediately. One need only give equal consideration to biblical *salvation* to gain a clearer understanding of the analogy as it relates to *transformation*. For example, *salvation* is not only instantaneous but also occurs in two other *stages*: you *are saved*, you are *being saved* and you *will be saved*. The Bible teaches this.

Why is this relevant for what we are discussing? It's relevant because arguments that fight against your true identity can easily surface when contemplating transformation. You may already be programmed from past teachings you have to *wait this thing out* before you can be *One New Dude*. This is not true as it relates to being a new creature. For perfection; sure. On the other hand, if you are in Christ you are new… period! God has been telling you and continues to tell you—via this book and based upon scripture—because you are likely to not be fully persuaded, at times.

For example, if a carnal thought enters your mind, perhaps you do what is wise and commanded by God. Perhaps you take the thought captive to the obedience of Christ. Yet, you might get shaken up a bit over the matter and begin to question your identity for having the thought. What's likely going on is your faith is being tested. These are the times when you must be decisive regarding who you are.

Your energy needs to be spent wielding your sword of truth against the lies of the enemy and any lack of faith. It's not to be spent beating up yourself for occupying a body which is yet to be redeemed. Accept the fact *you are transformed* as *One New Dude*. Also settle on the *fact* that even though changes are still occurring, the sacrifice of Jesus secures your singular identity in Him when you accepted it. *Your humanness is not your sinful nature/old man. He is gone for good!*

Let's pull up another verse. Notice how God, through Paul, exhorts those who *are new creations* but are acting *contrary* to their divine nature:

"for you are still fleshly. For since there is jealousy and strife among you, are you not fleshly, and are you not walking like mere men?"
~ 1 Corinthians 3:3 NASB

Christians walking *as men, being carnal* at times illustrates an important point. As *One New Dude*, unless you expire immediately after being born again, you will experience *progressive sanctification*. Just because you will make mistakes as God shines light into some dark areas of your humanness, you are nevertheless confirmed by God's Word as being *One New Dude*; a *transformed* sinner now a *son!* So, Paul's reasoning is God has transformed these souls into new creations, but they are still behaving as if they haven't *turned the key*.

Consider for a moment the *One New Dude* who just got born-again. There may be specific details regarding what Jesus actually accomplished for him at the Cross and yet, those details remain uncovered. Perhaps the details were not so carefully examined or taken in faith, as was the situation in my case.

What should be fair to say as being typically comprehended is:

"I am a sinner in need of a saving lifeline. I'm ecstatic Jesus has provided it!"

This is oftentimes the extent of it and reasonably so. Additionally, new creatures in Christ are not yet likely to have cracked open a Bible on a consistent basis. Oftentimes, they were just given one upon making a commitment to Jesus or have yet to pick one up for themselves. Even those who *have* cracked open and studied the Bible—whether it be over a short or long period of time—are still being washed by the water of it. There's plenty to *discover* and plenty of *change to come* as a result of this washing.

Therefore, do not let others or the enemy confuse you as God washes you and works in you. You may have been a sinner but now you are a *saint* and a *son*. Simply asserting a believer is *carnal* or still *walks as mere men* doesn't require, therefore, this person is carrying around a sinful nature. There are reasonable explanations as to what the case could be. For the sake of brevity, I'll only suggest two:

1) The *One New Dude* is still coming into a full realization of who they are, in Jesus.

2) The *One New Dude* still has indwelling sin, but *not* a

sinful nature. *(Otherwise, Christ didn't cut the sinful nature away as Colossians 2 tells us He did, and we know the Bible is truthful.)*

Some have argued you couldn't possibly be *One New Dude* right now because *transformation (metamorpho/omai)* must always be a progressive, gradual process.

However, consider this. The event that supernaturally recreates an *old dude* as *One New Dude is transformation*. Just because you are *being transformed*—this does not forbid you from *already being transformed* when God is involved. Again, is there anything too hard for the Lord?

Consider the text:

"Therefore, if anyone is in Christ, he is a new creation. The old has passed away; behold, the new has come."
~ 2 Corinthians 5:17 ESV

Even if the divine nature is argued to be some form of *addition*, you still have to subtract the *old man/sinful nature/old self*, because God has indicated it is already crucified. Do you trust Him on this? Please…trust Him! You must choose to take Him at his Word if you are to walk in true newness of the life. God has sacrificially arranged all of this for you. This is unmatched by anything the world is trying to offer to you! It's unlike any message which says you have to do something Jesus has already done for you. *Jesus has everything you need and God is showing you new and amazing stuff, right now!*

Now—these next four points, like the rest of this book, are an imperfect attempt to reason out some of the finer details of your identity in Jesus.

Nevertheless, even as an *imperfect* attempt, I trust you will benefit greatly from the revelation available. The overall objective of these points is to present a smaller biblical case to tie in with the larger biblical case, as to why you are *One New Dude*. Not *One New Dude* who's been fighting against an *already crucified old self*, but what I would suggest is the *genuine One New Dude* God created to reign, through Christ.

So, here we go. *Salvation, crucifixion and baptism* are used below to make contrasts with *transformation*. They will further support all of the other strong evidence as to why the believer is freed of their old, sinful nature.

Salvation: *Immediate, as well as progressive/gradual - you are* saved, you are being saved, you will be saved.

Transformation: *Immediate, as well as progressive/gradual*

Proposed reasoning: Transformation can be immediate, as well as gradual/progressive, without violating scripture.

If a believer instantly becomes a new creation as scripture states, then this is immediate transformation. Consider the basic example of a caterpillar transformed into a butterfly. We are told above "if anyone is in Christ, he is a *new creation."* Observe the *present* tense: *"is"* a new creation.

Some might say, *"Well see, there ya go! It's a process. It takes this butterfly time to be transformed."*

Fair enough. It does take some time; perhaps as little as two weeks.[47]

A reasonable question back to this person who disagrees with immediate transformation might be: *"Have you been a Christian for more than two weeks?"* If they have been, then why wouldn't they be the new creation after two weeks? Do they still not trust they are a butterfly?

In fairness, this last response would still not fully satisfy all contenders. The change is a gradual change, albeit a mere few weeks. Yet, don't throw the baby out with the bath water. We're not done!

The butterfly analogy was too good to pass up. God is telling you as *One New Dude* you are no longer the old person at all. You are *completely new!* God certainly sees the finished product, but He also sees the miracle of transformation which occurred the moment He *saved* and *sanctified* you. Once again, your job is to trust what God says.

Since the butterfly analogy won't entirely cut it for this exhortation that transformation *would include immediate change*, other examples in this book will have to suffice. Yet, let's just throw in another, for good measure:

> *"What's more, I am changing your name. It will no longer be Abram. Instead, you will be called Abraham, for you will be the father of many nations."*
> **~ Genesis 17:5 NLT**

God said it and it was done. *Boom!* Period. Abram was transformed into Abraham in a moment! In other words and my words, *"Abram, you thought you were always going to be Abram. Guess what? You are no longer the old person; you are now the new person. Abram is no more. Abraham is the now. Run with it. Cooperate with the P-G... the Pro-Gram, through faith."*

Did Abraham say ... *"That's a bit too much to believe, Lord. Are you serious? OK. I appreciate that, so here's what I'm gonna do. I'll go by Abraham now but I'll always know in my heart I'm really Abram. Will that work?* No! When you examine this text in context, Abraham doesn't say anything! He must have simply trusted what God said as fact! In other words and in my words: *"Roger that, Captain of my Soul! I'm good with it!"*

In light of this and other examples, isn't it reasonable to conclude God is in the business of transforming on the spot—creating, recreating, doing whatever He pleases?

As *One New Dude*, you are *transformed* immediately, as well as in a *progressive/gradual state*. This is fully consistent with your *immediate sanctification* as well as your *progressive sanctification*.

Therefore, based upon these considerations it's *reasonable* to conclude similar to *salvation*, the believer is transformed *immediately, progressively, and ultimately*. There is nothing precluding God from allowing for this. Nor should it place into error a believer who trusts such matches up with the truth.

Crucifixion: *One time event*, not a progressive, gradual or ongoing thing. It may have lasted several hours or more for each person, back when crucifixion was common. It was not a lifetime, though.

Additionally, when we look at scripture specific to the new creation, crucifixion is a done deal. It's always used in the past tense, contrary to what certain Bible commentators may indicate in commentaries below inspired text. *"Have been crucified"* is not to be translated into, *"I'm being crucified every day."* Scripture clearly states the believer's sinful nature *has been crucified*. This is also why Galatians 5:24 confirms this, by stating, *"those who belong to Christ Jesus have crucified the flesh."*

You are being *sanctified* every day. While this may *feel* like a never-ending *crucifixion* at times, it's not accurate nor is it biblical to take what God has said—lean upon our own understanding—and interpret it as a *daily* crucifixion. Crucifixion is *not* sanctification. If a new creation chooses to focus on *indwelling sin* rather than *sonship and sainthood*, which is a gift from God, then they are free to do so.

Nevertheless, you must seriously get away from this type of

thinking if you are to walk as *One New Dude*. Mixing covenants—old and new—is akin to putting new wine into old wineskins. It's not encouraged! God does not desire your wineskin burst.

Baptism: *One time event*, not gradual or progressive. Otherwise, an ongoing baptism could begin to look a lot like a drowning! We are baptized into Christ's death.[48] This is more evidence the old man/old self/sin nature is dead; not alive. The believer's position is their condition: New!

> *"Do not be conformed to this world, but <u>be transformed by the renewal of your mind</u>, that by testing you may discern what is the will of God, what is good and acceptable and perfect."*
> **~ Romans 12:2 ESV**

As an unsaved, unregenerate human being, you *previously* conformed to the patterns of this world. But this isn't you any longer. Jesus saved you!

However, it's reasonable to conclude however long you were conforming to the patterns of this world, it had an impact on how you thought, reasoned, and behaved.

As you begin to accept what God says about your true and new identity in Jesus, you should be left with a clearer understanding of the real, *One New Dude* God has re-created. He's a single-natured man with a biblical place to account for his sin, minus a nature Jesus dealt with at the Cross.

> *"Only let us <u>live up to</u> what we <u>have already attained</u>."*[49]
> **~Philippians 3:16 NIV**

You can still be humble in God's eyes, which is where it counts most, while accepting God's amazing grace. God isn't calling for you to hang your head low. The Pharisee didn't humble himself and act as if he needed Jesus. The tax collector, on other hand, did show where his heart was. It wasn't lifted up. He knew he needed God's mercy.

Don't get me wrong. You can still be a *jerk* while having accepted God's amazing grace. I wouldn't encourage this, though. Still, God's exhortation to you is to *live up to* what you *have already attained* because of Jesus.

God calls you and me to take on more than one thing at a time. For example, we're told the righteous are as bold as a lion.[50]

You are to be bold for Jesus. Does this mean you cannot be humble? Was Paul prideful and acting as if he was without sin just because he boldly preached the gospel? Of course not.

So you see you are called to live as a son, not a sinner. Drop the sinner focus. Focus on being a saint, a son. God calls you to be humble, but not at the expense of other scripture. To take humility so far you never challenge people who are lying and murdering for example, would not seem to be God's will. God calls you to be humble and to be bold enough to make disciples of all nations. He calls you to be a son and He tells you your sinful nature is crucified. It's not arrogant to take God at his Word. It's arrogant to *not* take God at his word. There's a difference between arrogance and knowing your value in God's eyes.

Do not fear what other people think. Just as you hold onto God's Word as you share his love and truth with unbelievers, so must you hold onto God's Word as you *live up to what you have already attained.* Don't apologize for having enough faith to trust what God says. Instead, encourage others to embrace that which Jesus has paid such a price. Jesus paid a high price for you to be *One New Dude.*

"What happened to our old man when we were saved? He was crucified. No one comes down from a cross alive. Our old man was destroyed. Second Corinthians 5:17 says 'old things have passed away.' The word for 'passed away' is *parerchomai*, which means 'to be removed' or 'perish.' There is no 'coexistence' agreement. Our old nature is not sharing our body with the new nature. The old nature is gone for good."
~ *Woodrow Kroll (Taken from, "The Joy of Belonging: Discovering Who You Are In Christ", by Woodrow Kroll p. 83* © *March 1999 by Back to the Bible Publishing. Used with permission of Back to the Bible Publishing.)*

Your Response

Based upon what you have learned about your nature and true identity, what is your response? What should it be in light of God's revelation to you?

Much time has been spent in an effort to dismantle the type of thinking holding you back from the true newness Jesus died for you to experience. Before you paint a house, you had better break out the scraper and chip away the old, jagged paint. Preparatory work is crucial to laying a proper foundation! This is why everything leading up to this has been necessary and time well spent!

If your thinking is askew on your true identity your daily and remaining earthly life will likely be askew, as well. With this in mind, continue to be encouraged as we move towards closing out your nature inventory.

You are Not in the Flesh

You are no longer in the flesh, Dude. Don't forget: Those who belong to Jesus *have crucified* the flesh. We've been through this. Be discouraged *not* should your thoughts drift into a direction that is more indicative of the old you than the new you. You are not condemned, so don't allow yourself to bite the baited hook of your enemy which is condemning you! There's no condemnation for those in Jesus! None! Satan wants you to listen to his lies. God gave you his Word to encourage you, which I'll do in my own words, filled with Christ's Spirit: *"I'm in you, now. I've rescued you. You are most definitely new and I am sanctifying you, with your every breath and thought. Take every thought captive to My obedience to the Father. Rest in Me."*

Check it out:

> *"because the mind set on the flesh is hostile toward God; for it does not subject itself to the law of God, for it is not even able to do so, and those who are in the flesh cannot please God. However, <u>you are not in the flesh</u> but in the Spirit, if indeed the Spirit of God dwells in you. But if anyone does not have the Spirit of Christ, he does not belong to Him."*
> ~ **Romans 8:7-9 NASB**

You couldn't be *"in the Spirit"* without the Holy Spirit indwelling you. So, if you received Christ you have all of God the Holy Spirit; not just part of Him. When you invited Him in, He didn't come to just give you *part* of Him. The same Spirit who raised Christ from the dead now lives in you, *New Dude!* It's his good pleasure to will and to work in you! Your duty is to *turn the key.*

> *"For God is working in you, giving you the desire and the power to do what pleases him."*
> **~ Philippians 2:13 NLT**

Your Divine Nature

> *"Put on your new nature, <u>created</u> to be like God--<u>truly righteous and holy</u>."*
> **~ Ephesians 4:24 NLT**

> *"Put on your <u>new nature</u>, and be renewed as you learn to know your Creator and become like him."*
> **~ Colossians 3:10 NLT**

Jesus is in you. The Spirit of Christ is in you. The *old self* is gone. Divine nature reigns. You are 100% dependent upon Christ. This is where the power and authority is. The sinner doesn't have this so they are *unredeemed* sinners. New creations are identified as *sons* and *daughters,* not *sinners.* Just because it's popular doesn't mean you have to fall in line with it. Fornication is popular, as well.

Remember: *son* not *sinner.* You may still sin, but sin doesn't reign. You reign through Jesus. God doesn't keep calling you a sinner after He saves you. He knows you understood; you came to the Cross. Unsaved people don't see the need to change their mind about their pride, their sin or about God. The Christian does. Sons reign, not sin. This is why God's emphasis is no longer on sin for the *One New Dude*, but sonship. Your identity is a son, not a sinner. Christ didn't save you so you could go around telling everybody you are a sinner. He saved you so you could tell all the sinners how great it is to be a son! He wants them in heaven with you!

SAVED SINNERS BECOME SONS & SAINTS

You and I don't *have* to sin. Just because you may sin at times doesn't mean sin ought to be your focus. What about forgiveness and righteousness? Which mindset is more indicative of accepting grace? Which *focus* will yield fruit in your life?

> *"For as he thinks in his heart, so is he:"*
> **~ Proverbs 23:7 AKJV**

Focusing on First John 1 is another conversation. Yet, while certainly nobody here is saying *New Dudes* never sin, God is not saying we are resigned to sin. To the contrary, sin is to be the exception; if at all. The Bible makes this clear.

Jesus said anyone who sins is a *slave* to sin. Are you a *slave to righteousness* or a *slave to sin?* If righteousness but you sin at times, does it mean you are a slave to sin and always have to sin? Of course not! If you are accentuating sin in your life, stop! Some say, *"Hey brother... whatever you feed will grow."* Great! I agree. Stop feeding the *identity of a sinner*, then! Focus on what Jesus has done instead of what you can achieve. It will never be enough to redirect the focus from Jesus to you. You should not labor in your identity or in earning God's favor as a son; *rest*. Talk about taking a burden from your shoulders! You will find it helpful and to your advantage to pick teams on these things.

For example, receive grace and accentuate what God has done and given to you by his Son, or... sit on the fence. Harbor in your mind the old you *and* the new you at the same time. God doesn't appear to want this for you. He told you to *throw off* the old man who has already been crucified:

> *"<u>throw off your old sinful nature</u> and your former way of life, which is corrupted by lust and deception."*
> **~ Ephesians 4:22 NLT**

The single-natured believer, which I would contend is what God re-created you as, understands he may still sin at times. He understands who he is, though. He's *not* divided. When you trust God and accept his gift that He has re-made you, your outlook will change. You will actually walk as *One New Dude* because you *actually believe* you *are One New Dude!* You have biblical permission to *throw off* the crucified, old sinful nature and walk as *One New Dude!* Try it! Step outside of your comfort zone and perhaps the theological box preventing you from discovering what God has done.

"Every good and perfect gift is from above, coming down from the Father of the heavenly lights, who does not change like shifting shadows." ~ **James 1:17** — this is one of those good and perfect things from above, to be sure! You have permission to reject any lie that whispers or even yells to you that you are not new! Old thoughts and lies creeping up are just lame attempts to persuade you to believe lies instead of God. Don't tolerate them! Use your Sword, like Jesus did![51]

Renewed in Knowledge

"and have put on the new self, which is being renewed in knowledge in the image of its Creator."
~ Colossians 3:10 NIV

"Put on your new nature, and be renewed as you learn to know your Creator and become like him."
~ Colossians 3:10 NLT

A great example of what God actually planned for you, as *One New Dude*.
- God tells you are *One New Dude* (a *new creation*, in Christ.)
- God tells you to now put on the *One New Dude*, because this is your true identity. God is allowing for you to discover it. Asking, seeking, and knocking are consistent with the exhortation of Christ. God knew when you were going to be saved and transformed into *One New Dude*. God knew when you would receive grace and be brought back into relationship, redeemed and adopted as his child.
- Is the Holy Spirit the Spirit of Christ? You betcha He is.
- Does He live in you? You betcha He does.
- Do you *believe it* and *will you walk in this faith* every day? (Otherwise, how can one claim to have faith?)
- Consider this: You do have faith! God has given you faith

and God's plan is for your faith to grow!

What's going to grow your faith more? Trusting in what God tells you about *what went down* and is going on, or—holding onto the *old* while trying to hold onto the *new?*

My friend, the monkey could not get its hand out of the jar when it would not let go of the stuff!

In your case, Jesus is indicating a similar thing to you: *New wine don't go in no old wineskins, yo!*[52] You must let go of the old. In with the new! Decide. The new only becomes a reality when you *turn the key* on what God says because until you do this, you are never going to be persuaded yourself! You'll constantly be in doubt. Doubt is not good when it comes to God's promises! Amen? *Hallelujah!*

Jesus said: *"All authority has been given to Me in heaven and on earth."*[53] When you received the Spirit of Christ, the Holy Spirit came to live in you. Now…

Do you live, or does Christ live? One is dead my friend and I can tell you… it isn't Jesus! *So who lives?* Jesus said He is *"the life"*. If He lives in you what do you have? You have *life*; spiritual life! His name is Jesus! Jesus is not divided, nor is He sharing space with another nature. He *is* the nature in you; the divine nature. You are *One New Dude!*

> "To them God has chosen to make known among the Gentiles the glorious riches of this mystery, which is Christ in you, the hope of glory."
> **~ Colossians 1:27**

Again, who lives—the sinful nature—or Jesus? Who lives according to God? Complaints? Questions? Refusals? *Who lives?* You say, *"Jesus!"* You were purchased with his precious blood. Isn't this a fantastic reality and reminder?

So, let me ask you. Is it time to rise up in Jesus? Speak God's truth when Satan or his demons whisper ongoing lies to you. Establish and reinforce sin doesn't rule. Rather, the King of Glory rules your being! Speak verbally and/or non-verbally. This is warfare! You are not divided but instead—united with the Holy Spirit!

Is it time for your faith to be active or passive? Is it time for you—from your very core, the spirit man—to stand upon the promises of God? Is it time to establish once and for all you are *not scattered or confused* about who you are, *One New Dude*?

It is time, my friend. It is time! You have God's permission to realize who He has recreated you to be.

Truth or Consequences

If you keep claiming and fighting against a *sinful nature* Jesus took care of, this begs the question: is Satan deceiving you? God says one thing, Satan says another. God reveals it's dead and for you personally, to get rid of it. Satan whispers to you, *"It's not dead, you're not new and you can't get rid of it!"* Who do you trust, today?

If the *key isn't turned* on the old man being crucified and it's even further exacerbated by refusing to throw it off, it might be worth considering the following, brief illustration. By the way, my understanding of this illustration[54] is given in the context of Romans 7:24, which says:

"Wretched man that I am! Who will deliver me from this body of death?"
~ Romans 7:24 ESV

Be that as it may, we have already established there are valid reasons to make a distinction between the *flesh/sinful nature* and the *flesh/humanness/physical body*. Therefore, I am pointing you to this illustration for a reason other than how it has been cited by others.

Rather, it will be for the same reason I have been pointing you to numerous other examples and illustrations. That is this: to have plenty of reasons to leave behind the old and walk in the new! Let it further encourage and motivate you in God's will for your life. Here's the illustration:

Apparently, there's been some type of report regarding a tribe which originates near Tarsus, where Paul was born. This tribe would dish out a horrifying penalty to murderers. What they would do is strap their victim back-to-back, including both the shoulders and the arms. The tribe would then force the murderer out of the community. While wandering, the decay of the victim's corpse would begin to transfer to the murderer's living body. Slowly but surely, the decay would overcome the murderer, resulting in death.

In this horrific example, the murderer couldn't get rid of what had been strapped to his/her body. Nobody was around to help. For whatever reason, they were isolated or nobody was able or willing to help them to be freed from this corpse.

Conversely, in your reality as a Christ-Follower, God has given you the ability to do *all* things through Christ! Not only has Christ crucified your sinful nature, He has given you a measure of faith, your very own free will and God the Holy Spirit to walk out the rest of your days *without a sinful nature!* You don't need to carry the thing around any longer—if you still are!

Let's go for more word pictures. You of course are not a snake or a locust, but we're going to use the two as examples. *Don't recoil too quickly!* Remember, Jesus did instruct us to *"be wise as serpents, but innocent as doves."*[55] So, here's just another little something to consider. They are not *perfectly harmonious* examples but hopefully you'll grab hold of the analogous exhortation.

At some point, the snake's *old skin* is dead. Does the snake leave it on or is it *intentional* on getting rid of that thing?

What about those *cicadas* or those locusts that make all the noise in the trees during later summer months? What's the deal with all of the commotion, you might ask? It's the occasion of these locusts crawling out of their nymphal skin,[56] leaving it far behind!

Metaphorically, you are to throw the old nature that's already crucified... *off!* It no longer defines you; Christ does. The sinful nature that once defined you has been replaced by a new nature, empowered by God the Holy Spirit. *Not a small thing!* You are a recipient of God's promises. You are chosen! Even though it appears you chose Jesus, ultimately you have found Jesus chose you. You were purchased by His precious blood. *Hallelujah!*

> *"You did not choose Me but I chose you, and appointed you that you would go and bear fruit, and that your fruit would remain, so that whatever you ask of the Father in My name He may give to you."*
> **~ John 15:16 NASB**

By the way, in the snake analogy the snake is still the same old snake, even though it shed its skin. That is why this analogy is limited. Hopefully, it still illustrates the point. What you are throwing off is your old identity, which Jesus made new. That's a big deal! God recreated you. You weren't born entirely in God's image. You were reborn in God's image. This is why Jesus came—to give you second birth!

Now that you have had a supernatural birth—born of God—you have a new identity. Period! You must be persuaded or you are never going to persuade others. Did Jesus die for this to occur or for something better to occur? *Correct!* Jesus came that you would have life and have it more abundantly! Someone lift their eyes and thank Jesus for all He is doing, right now. *Thank you, Jesus!*

Summary

The Holy Spirit Leads You to Truth
Let the opinion of others be confirmed by Holy Scripture. Just because you may have always understood scripture to say one thing—this does not exclude the possibility it may be saying another. Allow yourself to seek God persistently, especially on matters of: *Pure grace, Christ's finished work on the cross and your identity in Him.*

The Importance of "Turning the Key"
Scripture does indeed support the *"truster of Christ"* as having only one nature, a divine nature. When we talk about nature we are talking about identity; who you actually *are*. Have you *turned the key?* Consider some of the main verses we highlighted:

- **Galatians 5:24**
- **Romans 6:4**
- **Romans 6:6**
- **Colossians 2:11**
- **Colossians 2:13**
- **Galatians 2:20**

Assign Some Buckets
Oftentimes, breakthrough is a matter of child-like faith and holding your ground in it. If God wasn't interested in increasing your faith, there would be no challenges to your faith in life or when absorbing God's Word. Utilizing some form of bucket system might just help

you to throw something in the trash, once and for all.

In this case of the flesh *already being crucified*, I can promise you settling this *flesh/sinful nature* matter has changed my life. What's even more celebratory is God endorses it. He started the whole thing! He planned and executed this plan. He's way ahead of you to no surprise! Jesus goes ahead of you—into Galilee. Let me continue to encourage you to break free of trying to line up with what is popular if you have to do so at the expense of clear revelation from God. Never coming into a realization or being persuaded of the *One New Dude* God has arranged on your behalf, in Christ, is something I'd never desire for you. As you allow God to place people in your life to teach you and guide you, make sure you are not automatically dismissing any who would bring something different to the table for you to consider. As you test everything, make sure you don't get so comfortable in your current positions you neglect to allow God to stretch your faith. As I've indicated before, your *true identity* hangs in the balance.

Reasoning with Alternate Views

You and I are commanded to treat everyone with respect. While each of us can fall short at times, join me in encouraging one another in the Lord, even when we may hold to a different view. In this case, reasonable arguments and discussions can arise on such interesting topics which would include one's *nature* inventory. Those in Christ are one in Christ. We comprise his body. Identity and how it is understood matters—so it's fair to say it's worth discussing. Reasonable responses have been offered to what might be some popular arguments against holding to *one-naturism*. While the responses and proposed reasoning will not satisfy all, let them serve as encouragement to you as you discover your true identity—when you trust what God says.

The Flesh

When it comes to the *flesh*, get intentional about drawing a distinction between your *crucified and buried old man* and your *unredeemed physical body*. Your unredeemed body is a liability you must deal with until the glorious exchange is made. As you consider everything mentioned regarding *humanness* or the *flesh*, another definition unmentioned but still worthy to be considered is: that part of you which is *yet-to-be-changed*. You and I may not understand or know how to explain how *all* of the supernatural details have been worked out, but you certainly can bank upon what God has said. If you belong to Jesus your sinful nature has been crucified. It's a done deal. God said it. What is your response? Hopefully, you now recognize you have permission to walk in newness. Perhaps a newness you have never experienced—all because you trusted what God says.

> *"So if the Son sets you free, you will be free indeed."*
> **~ John 8:36 NIV**

Sanctification

Understanding and reminding yourself you are righteous because you have received God's gift of salvation and righteousness through faith is critical. Refuse to panic over anything, period! Jesus indicated worrying wasn't going to do anything for you. Even more to the point, allow yourself to experience the grace God has bestowed upon you as you work out your salvation. Your enemy is defeated and so is the power of sin in your life. When you are on board with this and refuse to ever let your identity come into question, the enemy's lies are stomped out. Jesus never forgot who He was when Satan cunningly said, *"If you are the Son of God…"* Neither should you forget who you are as you journey through this battlefield of lies and temptation. By the way, your citizenship is in *Heaven*, not here!

Consider Some Math

Once Fallen. You were born with a fallen/sinful nature which consisted of a dead spirit and physical body carrying the cancer of sin.

Born Again. You were reborn when you received Christ. As with Paul, the fallen and sinful nature which once identified you—*died*. The Spirit of Christ *lives*. The *you* who lives—which is Christ in you—occupies an unredeemed physical body. This body carries the cancer of surviving sin as it awaits its own redemption.

Replacement. Subtracting a sinful nature and replacing it with a divine nature corresponds directly to identity; old man to new man. The physical body does not determine your identity. While sin finds its base of operation within the members of the physical body, an old nature still died and a new nature now reigns, through Jesus. The physical body is not your *identity*. It's a temporary *tent*. The real you—

the partaker of the divine nature—lives within this body. The body is not eternal but you are. Your redeemed body, which is forthcoming, will be better suited for you. Unlike your current body it will be *incorruptible*.

Acknowledging and living with the faith that *what God says is true* about this matter will directly impact how you view grace. If Christ died to give you the results this math reveals, then be encouraged to receive God's grace, completely! Walk in the true newness this grace offers, as it directly relates to your true identity.

Try this: *"I'm One New Dude. I'm not confused about it. I don't have a split personality. God said it and I trust Him. I'm dead, Christ lives in me. Any remaining sinful deeds that stem from either my physical body or previous nature are being put to death by Christ's Spirit in me. He has set me free! He is my Defender. He's my Victor. I live, yet not I, but it's Christ in me who lives!"*

The Sonsets Free!

"I believe it is a serious misunderstanding to think of the believer as having both an old and new nature. Believers do not have dual personalities... there is no such thing as an old nature in the believer."
— *(John MacArthur, Freedom From Sin, pp. 31-32)*

"The biggest difficulty in believing that sin is a vanquished foe is the constant conflict believers have with sin. When you destroy people's convenient theological categories by teaching what God really says—that there is only one nature in the believer— many don't know how to respond."
— *(John MacArthur, Freedom From Sin, p. 52)*

"According to Romans 6, the old nature represents a person before salvation, who exists solely in a state of habitual sinfulness. The new nature, however, describes a regenerate man who lives a life of righteousness and holiness that is honoring to God."
— *(John MacArthur, Freedom From Sin, p.43)*

"being 'dead to sin' means that 'I no longer possess a sin nature.'"
— *(John MacArthur, Freedom From Sin, p. 50)*

"Who was I before? Bob George in Adam. That man is dead and gone; he will never exist again."
— *Bob George*
Taken from: CLASSIC CHRISTIANITY
Copyright © 1989 by Harvest House Publishers
Eugene, Oregon 97402
www.harvesthousepublishers.com
Used by Permission.

Why should you change your mind & your life?
Solid Reason #3:
You have
One Divine Nature!

Jesus told them, "This is the only work God wants from you: Believe in the one he has sent."
~ John 6:29 NLT

Ask, Seek, Knock.
Stop doubting and believe!

Life Application

1. Have you come to Jesus for your new nature?

2. As *One New Dude*, do you trust God has replaced your old nature with a new, divine nature? Has Satan put a question mark where God has put a period?

3. Are you able to say the same as Mary? *"May it be to me as you have said."*

4. What changes might you make to align yourself with God's truth?

PERSONAL NOTES

PART 3

Chapter 5

PROJECT:

Righteousness Inventory

Isn't it amazing how your cup is overflowing with the goodness of God because of Jesus? To think there's more to get excited about than we've already covered is astonishing! As we continue to wrap things up, it only seems fitting we take a quick inventory of an eternally relevant topic: your *righteousness* in Christ, as *One New Dude*.

Let's have a look at how righteousness is commonly defined if you were to look it up in a dictionary, as well as how righteousness pertains to you as God's child. We'll also briefly consider the contrast between you as *One New Dude* and those not yet regenerated by God's Spirit.

Continue to be filled with joy over what Jesus has done on your behalf. God himself made a way out of heaven to rescue you from the horrific penalty of judgment and condemnation. You crossed *from death* over *to life* when you were born again of the Spirit of God. That's supernatural and worth getting excited about!

Rags to Riches

Looking at the term *righteousness* we typically observe it being associated with accepted standards of morality.[57] This might be why many consider themselves to be righteous in their own eyes. In our society it's common for people to consider themselves to be *good*, or *righteous*.

Perhaps the reason for this is because they have never met Jesus. When comparing themselves to their neighbor they feel pretty good about themselves. Watching the evening news or comparing themselves to others, the temptation presents itself and many have bitten the baited hook of *self-righteousness*. In having the wrong guidance system of truth, masses of people slide down the wide and slippery slope to hell. Thinking they are a *good person*—or at least a *good enough person* to get into heaven—reveals their lack of insight when it comes to God's righteousness and eternal truth. God tells us Satan is active behind it all:

> *"in whose case the god of this world has blinded the minds of the unbelieving so that they might not see the light of the gospel of the glory of Christ, who is the image of God."*
> **~ 2 Corinthians 4:4**

By now, you have likely come to understand God's standard is perfection. When you became aware Christ was your only lifeline you grabbed it! That was a wise move, *One New Dude!* There exists no wiser move than this anywhere, at any time. In your moment of trust and conversion, you reached the perfection which was and is required of you before a holy God. Consider the requirement put forth by Jesus:

> *"You therefore must be perfect, as your heavenly Father is perfect."*
> **~ Matthew 5:48 ESV**

What did you have before you surrendered to Jesus and what do others have before or without a personal surrendering to Jesus? We read in God's Word:

> *"We are all infected and impure with sin. When we display our righteous deeds, they are nothing but filthy rags. Like autumn leaves, we wither and fall, and our sins sweep us away like the wind."*
> **~ Isaiah 64:6 NLT**

Marinate in this for a moment. Let it sink in even if you've visited and understood this revelation, previously. The more you observe the stark contrast, the more likely and consistently you will carry a grateful heart. Never forget from what Jesus has saved you. Isn't it crazy and yet sobering when God uses *bloody menstrual rags* to reveal just how offensive it is for any human being to approach him apart from Jesus?

God indicates when a person trusts in their own righteousness it's like holding a pile of menstrual rags and saying, *"Here, God… how's this for you? I'm cleared of all charges for my crimes against you, right? Will you let me in, now?"* It's as if there's no response required to the finished work at Calvary. Rather than live a surrendered life of faith, the moral or religious person is blinded and overlooks the simplicity of the gospel message:

> *"I do not set aside the grace of God, for if righteousness could be gained through the law, Christ died for nothing!"*
> **~ Galatians 2:21 NIV**

What's more, as we come into the awareness of who Jesus is—*God in the flesh*—how much more foolish is the rejection of a life devoted to Jesus, in faith? To reject the option of following Jesus is to reject the option of knowing and being led by God, himself! Jesus is no ordinary Man. He tells us many times and in many different ways. Here's just a brief look by way of reminder:

JESUS SPEAKS: "*Have I been so long with you, and yet you have not come to know Me, Philip? He who has seen Me has seen the Father; how can you say, 'Show us the Father'?*"
~ John 14:9 NASB

As *One New Dude*, God made you aware your so-called righteousness was never going to cut it. He offered you a type of righteousness which exists nowhere else in this galaxy: the *righteousness from God through faith in Christ*. When you accepted *this* righteousness, God made you perfect in his eyes. He sees Jesus when He looks at you! God sees you as perfectly righteous. Instead of the stench of filthy menstrual rags you are a sweet aroma to Him. The fragrance of Christ!

> "*Our lives are a Christ-like fragrance rising up to God. But this fragrance is perceived differently by those who are being saved and by those who are perishing.*"
> ### ~ 2 Corinthians 2:15 NLT

He made you righteous! You let go of anything you could offer up for yourself in your defense and essentially said:

"*The blood? I'll take it, Lord! Graft me into the family! I'm a wandering soul with many pending crimes. I've lied. I've put many things before You. I'm an idolater and immoral in both thought and deed. Save me and adopt me as your child, please?*"

As it was way back in time with Abraham, you believed God and God credited your account with righteousness! Even though you *weren't* perfect when God saw you, He put into motion a divine transaction when you *turned the key*. He credited your faith as righteousness. Oh, how happy is the man whose lawless deeds are no longer remembered!

The divine transaction occurred between you and your heavenly Father when you placed your trust in Christ. It was a thing called, *imputation,* or *imputed righteousness*.[58] Imputation is God's method of dealing with your crimes against him and his holy, moral law. Since the wage for sin is death in God's system of justice, God sent Jesus to establish a new covenant between God and you. Jesus willingly answered the call.

In this new covenant and through faith, the Father takes Christ's sinless life and imputes it to you. It's as if your entire life is and has been lived perfectly. Christ—on the other hand— absorbed God's wrath at the Cross. It was as if Christ was guilty of all of your crimes and God poured his punishment out and upon Jesus. He who knew no sin became sin. Still today, people question God's goodness! Can you believe it?

> *"God made him who had no sin to be sin for us, so that in him we might become the righteousness of God."*
> **~ 2 Corinthians 5:21 NIV**

> *"But now the righteousness of God has been manifested apart from the law, although the Law and the Prophets bear witness to it—the righteousness of God through faith in Jesus Christ for all who believe."*
> **~ Romans 3:21-22 ESV**

So, you continue to get a feel for the magnitude of Christ's sacrifice on your behalf. When you received Christ's payment for your crimes, you turned from going your own way and instead followed Him. Do you see how everything God gives you in the new covenant empowers you to walk as *One New Dude?* You get the new heart, the new mind, the new nature, the new spirit and a new righteousness. Continually walking in the awareness of how God sees you is God's will! You are not to walk as if you are the same, old person. This is not the plan. There is no faith or humility in this! Don't allow popular opinion to sway you on this matter.

As pointed out earlier, you are no longer a sinner. A sinner practices sin and is a slave to sin, according to Jesus. Are you a slave to sin, or a slave to righteousness? You must choose and God laid the path out for you in the new covenant. You are to walk in this. He said you are righteous! You are a son—a slave of righteousness. Have you or are you going to turn the key on this one, or will you settle for second best? Don't settle! You are righteous and God has no problem with you telling other people why you are righteous. All glory goes to the King of kings, Jesus—and you are to let your light shine before men!

Jesus is the only one who solved the problem of man's righteousness problem before a holy God. That's why we worship him, fall at his feet and point others to him. He's the only One who can fix their problem.

Summary

God has set you apart from those who lean upon their own righteousness, mere church attendance or good deeds. As one who trusts Christ, God has already declared you innocent. You don't have to wait until you get to heaven for any of this. God has empowered you with eternal truth so you can walk *right now* as *One New Dude!* Check it out:

> *"By this is love perfected with us, so that we may have confidence for the day of judgment, because <u>as he is so also are we in this world</u>."*
> **~ 1 John 4:17 ESV**

Those walking around this planet never having come to a saving faith in Jesus Christ do not possess the righteousness you possess. You aren't better than them but you are certainly better off! It's tragic for them, but you have a lot to celebrate!

You can celebrate as you *hate* your life for the sake of Christ's gospel. Those same people who hold filthy menstrual rags before our holy God may actually come to know him by your love. It's Jesus who lives in you and He wants *out* and all over them![59]

Keep in mind: as *One New Dude* your righteousness in Christ is not a feeling—it is a fact. You can tell the Christian from the non-Christian based upon where their trust lies and if there is fruit in their life, as a result. The very fact your trust is in Jesus changes *once for all time* your relationship *to* and *with* God. With God's gift of repentance and imputed righteousness, Christ in you produces a life of holiness. Righteousness changes everything *forever* and it's because of Jesus your heavenly Father is no longer counting your sins against you.

Whereas you used to hold a pile of filthy rags in an attempt to please your Creator, Jesus has removed those filthy rags and provided you with the only righteousness you will ever need: *One righteousness—from God—through faith in Christ, alone!*

Why should you change your mind & your life?
Solid Reason #4:
You have One Righteousness!

Ask, Seek, Knock.
Stop doubting and believe!

Life Application

1. Have you come to Jesus for your new righteousness, or are you still holding onto filthy menstrual rags?

2. As *One New Dude*, have you been diligent to enter into the rest Christ offers? Is your focus whether or not you had a good day, spiritually—instead of the righteousness of Jesus, which belongs to you?

3. What changes might you make to align yourself with God's truth?

PERSONAL NOTES

Chapter 6

PROJECT:
Spirit Inventory

Many people don't seem to pay much attention to their spirit as it relates to the *condition* of the spirit *(dead or alive)*, do they? As you observe the things around you, have you noticed the massive amount of people wrapped up in mere church attendance, mere morality, New Age spirituality, tarot card readings and idol worship? Man's craving for spiritual things and to worship *something* is certainly evident. Observe collectors or sports *fans*. The blood gets pumping, but is it for Jesus?

People are spiritual because at the end of the day, we are *spirit*, soul and body. It's the *One New Dude* though, who has the only thing that matters in the end: *spiritual life*. And it's all because of Jesus!

> *"Whoever has the Son has life; whoever does not have the Son of God does not have life."*
> ~ 1 John 5:12 ESV

In this brief inventory, you're going to be encouraged as we take a closer look at your spirit. Your celebration continues because as we have discussed, Jesus has *jumped* your spirit and made it alive! Remember the dead car battery? You don't have this any longer! Jesus came so you would have life and have it *abundantly*. Who knows how to give abundant life more than the *Author of Life, himself?*

Breathe

When you consider the spirit and these other components of your being, you'll notice they have something in common. They are all *intangible*. Although distinct, soul and spirit are often used interchangeably. I have observed *heart* and *mind* used interchangeably, as well. When you consider all of what we are putting together in this book, there's a lot to consider when we examine the invisible parts which make up your being. While Bible teachers and other Christians have different ways of describing these intangibles, God's revelation still allows for us to make some insightful observations.

Interestingly enough, the human spirit encompasses much of what we've been looking at in the respective chapter inventories. Your spirit would include your intellect, fears, emotions, passions and creativity.[60] You can see how there's some overlap with other intangible components of your being. We won't be able to make a comprehensive study of all of these components, so let's grab what we can and be edified in the truth!

As *One New Dude*, when you invited Christ in, it's important to understand God did *not* give you a spirit of fear. He gave you the same Spirit who raised Christ from the dead! This is the same Spirit who gives *life* to your mortal body.

Marinating in the reality you are indeed a spiritual being, let's take a quick look at how it all began.

Does *life* come from *non-life?* Certainly not! This is why we read:

> "then the Lord God formed the man of dust from the ground and breathed into his nostrils the breath of life, and the man became a living creature."
> **~ Genesis 2:7 ESV**

In the Hebrew
"neshamah" is: "breath"[61]
In the Greek
"pneuma" is: wind, breath, spirit[62]

Let's jump directly into a word-picture to better establish what we've just covered.

The year was around 1990. During a Naval warship commissioning ceremony, I believe it was the Master of Ceremonies who made reference to the *unmanned* warship located directly behind the speaking platform. The ship was indeed impressive. Moored to the Mississippi pier, it was the most technologically advanced warship in the world.

Indicating to the crowd the ship was nothing more than a huge hunk of metal, cables and wires… the speaker gave the order for the crew to, *"Man the ship!"*

Upon the order, the crew immediately *double-timed* from the pier, up the ship's brow and onto the ship's weather decks. With the entire crew now on-board, the pile of well-organized metal, cable and wire had *come to life!*

Notice the parallel. When God formed man from the dust of the earth, he was lifeless. As the ship was a lifeless vessel, so was the vessel of man. Akin to the way the crew brought life to the lifeless vessel, so does God breathe into men of dust to give life to the vessel. It was the crew that *animated* the once *lifeless* ship. It was and always is God who breathes life into man, animating an otherwise lifeless vessel.

The *spirit* then, is indicative of man's *inner, dynamic force*. Your spirit animates you towards and into a specific direction. This explains further why you consistently *followed* your flesh into sinful thoughts and activity when your spirit was dead. Now that your spirit is alive as *One New Dude*, your direction is that of being led by the Spirit:

> *"For all who are led by the Spirit of God are children of God."*
> **~ Romans 8:14 NLT**

More than this and as we have discussed, it's the presence of God's Spirit who gives life to a *fallen* human being. God's Word tells us man is *spiritually dead* as a result of Adam's sin. Unlike the soul *without* an anchor, you can rejoice as *One New Dude*. God the Holy Spirit *regenerated* you and has given you spiritual life, in Jesus!

Marked

In these times which appear to be the actual *end times*, there's coming a *mark* which is prophesied. Without it, one will not be able to buy or sell. As you have likely been made aware, God reveals receiving this mark is beyond detrimental. The mark is commonly referred to as, *"the mark of the beast."* We read:

> *"And the smoke of their torment rises for ever and ever. There is no rest day or night for those who worship the beast and his image, or for anyone who receives the mark of his name."*
> ~ **Revelation 14:11 NIV**

God has been telling the end from the beginning for a very long time. It's reasonable to conclude this mark is not far away. You can see the evidence building as electronic tracking devices are inserted into not only animals, but human beings as well.

Conversely, as *One New Dude,* you are clearly on the other side of the spectrum. You have already been marked…by Jesus! You have been marked by and for God, sealed with the Holy Spirit. God has given you *his* Spirit as a deposit for things to come! Whether you've heard it before or not, this is an amazing truth for you to grab hold of each and every day!

> *"And you also were included in Christ when you heard the word of truth, the gospel of your salvation. Having believed, you were marked in him with a seal, the promised Holy Spirit, who is a deposit guaranteeing our inheritance until the redemption of those who are God's possession—to the praise of his glory."*
> ~ **Ephesians 1:13-14 NIV**

Testing

"So, JZ! How in the world can you tell me I have *one* spirit? I've been fully cognizant of the math the whole way through this little chapter and so far I have *my spirit* plus *God's Spirit* as *One New Dude*. The last time I checked 1+1=2!"

Oh? Hopefully, you weren't thinking such a thing. If you weren't, bravo! You pass! If you *were* falling back into simple math, allow me to refresh your memory. It was in Chapter 4 where we had a glance at some of God's *Kingdom math*, remember? We have another example, here.

In God's Kingdom your *human spirit* plus *God's Holy Spirit* equals *one!* 1+1=1. Not convinced, yet? Let's get convinced. Let's get intentional! Let's get so wrapped up in Jesus you discover a *singular* focus and awareness in the Lord you have never experienced:

> *"But the person who is joined to the Lord is one spirit with him."*
> **~ 1 Corinthians 6:17 NLT**

> *"The Spirit himself bears witness with our spirit that we are children of God,"*
> **~ Romans 8:16 ESV**

Intimacy: *"in-to-me-see."* That's right *One New Dude!* This is an intimacy which far exceeds any human relationship. The Lord Jesus sees right into every single person's heart, whether they are joined with him or not. The beautiful thing about *your* situation is you have become *one in spirit* with the Lord. Do you realize how astonishing this is? *Marinate in it! Celebrate it!* This is why you were created. To walk with your God, as *one spirit!* This stuff is crazy… and true! *It's crazy true!*

Summary

Always remember: every single person exists because God breathed into Adam's nostrils. Life cannot come from non-life! Rejoice in the fact you have the Son of God, *Jesus Christ*, who is *the life*. Pray for those around you who do not have the Son so they too might inherit eternal life. Share God's love with them as you let Jesus get out of you and all over them!

Continually remind yourself God has marked you and set you aside for his plan and purposes. Know God's down-payment on your guaranteed inheritance as a son is his Spirit residing within you. God *said it* and He isn't a man that He should lie. (Yes—God *became* a man but God *isn't* a man—He is Spirit. Amen?)

Finally, rest in knowing you *are* one spirit with God, through Christ. Remember what we covered earlier? God reveals to us through Paul: *you live yet not you*, but *Christ in you lives!* That's some more *serious, supernatural stuff* from our star-breathing Jesus!

"In the beginning was the Word, and the Word was with God, and the Word was God. He was with God in the beginning. Through him all things were made; without him nothing was made that has been made. In him was life, and that life was the light of men."
~ John 1:1-4 NIV

Why should you change your mind & your life?
Solid Reason #5:
*You are
One Spirit!*

Ask, Seek, Knock.
Stop doubting and believe!

Life Application

1. Have you come to Jesus to be united with God in spirit?

2. As *One New Dude*, are you affirming and re-affirming your constant communion with your Heavenly Father, through Jesus? Or, do you leave God behind until you think He should be part of whatever you are doing or thinking?

3. What changes might you make to be more aware of God's presence?

PERSONAL NOTES

Chapter 7

PROJECT:
Soul Inventory

The final phase of your *One New Dude* inventory investigates your *human soul*. It's an interesting note on which to end our inventory. Jesus appears to have placed the most emphasis upon how you look after this amazing miracle, which is *yourself* as a soul.

Got Soul?

C.S. Lewis indicated each person does not have a soul, but rather, *is a soul* that has a body.[63] Others have concluded you are a *spirit* who has a soul and a body. It's pretty tight competition because both seem to be biblically reasonable assessments.

When *soul* is used in the Bible, it refers to a person. It's been said your soul is the *software* part of your being, that part which is not physical.[64] Sometimes the soul and the spirit are used synonymously. However, even though there is overlap and similarities, the Holy Spirit has drawn a distinction between the two. So, we'll want to identify them as distinct, too:

> *"For the word of God is living and active and sharper than any two-edged sword, and piercing as far as the division of soul and spirit, of both joints and marrow, and able to judge the thoughts and intentions of the heart."*
> **~ Hebrews 4:12 NASB**

The revelation of God points to the soul being imperishable and eternal. Once it has departed from the unredeemed, temporary physical body it will reap what it has sown. If the soul rejected God's love in Christ, it will ultimately be condemned to pay for its sin eternally in hell. On the other hand, if the soul admitted its sinfulness and received God's forgiveness in Christ… that soul has been saved and will spend an eternity in bliss and the presence of God.[65]

Who is claiming ownership of all souls past, present and future? The Creator God, of course! Isn't it nice to know you aren't the product of mere chance, as if chance could result in a human being? You belong to God!

> *"Behold, all souls are mine; the soul of the father as well as the soul of the son is mine: the soul who sins shall die."*
> **~ Ezekiel 18:4 ESV**

It should also be mentioned by way of a reminder every soul requires atonement. Since God is a good Judge who is both merciful and just, his justice system requires payment for sin. The payment for sin is death. Sin carries with it a big price. One lie is a crime in God's court and enough to keep a soul from heaven!

    On that note, you probably remember what occurred in the Garden of Eden. When Adam and Eve ate of the *forbidden* fruit, blood had to be shed. Fig leaves weren't going to suffice. We see very early on there is indeed a wage for sin and this wage is *death*.

Catastrophic Coverage

Crimes against a holy God are a matter of life and death—not just in the here and now—but eternally!

In light of this, consider how awesome God has been to wayward souls from the very beginning. It was the holy Creator constantly going to great lengths in order to remain in relationship with you! We saw it with Adam and Eve and it continued as his plan unfolded in the Old Testament under the old covenant:

> *"For the life of the flesh is in the blood, and I have given it for you on the altar to make atonement for your souls, for it is the blood that makes atonement by the life."*
> **~ Leviticus 17:11 ESV**

As *One New Dude* you are blessed beyond measure under the *new* covenant! In this covenant, God continues to provide atonement for the souls of men. Whosoever calls upon Jesus will be saved in this new covenant. Jesus Christ is the only way because He's the only One who fixed the problem! You get to wake up with a smile on your face every day because when you were still not yet *One New Dude*, Christ was already handling the Father's business in order to rescue you from your many crimes against God:

> *"He himself is the sacrifice that atones for our sins--and not only our sins but the sins of all the world."*
> **~ 1 John 2:2 NLT**

> *"For Christ died for sins once for all, the righteous for the unrighteous, to bring you to God. He was put to death in the body but made alive by the Spirit,"*
> **~ 1 Peter 3:18 NIV**

Notice the continual pursuit of God to make atonement for your soul. *Astonishing, isn't it?* He holds your breath in his very hand, your heart beats without batteries and you are a precious soul to Him. He formed you in your mother's womb and you are fearfully and wonderfully made![66] When you had gone astray, Christ came as your Good Shepherd and tracked you down! Remember when He left the ninety-nine other sheep to find you in the ditch? Is Jesus not amazing? He certainly thinks you are worth pursuing, dying for, rising, then throwing you over his shoulders to take into his eternal, green pastures. You must be pretty special to for Jesus to do all of this!

Summary

The Creator of the universe breathed and made man a living soul. He owns all souls. Jesus reasoned with all people when He asked the question:

> *"And what do you benefit if you gain the whole world but lose your own soul?"*
> **~ Mark 8:36 NLT**

As *One New Dude*, you are *a spirit* who has *one soul!* You are unique not only because of your fingerprint and DNA—but also because you called upon Jesus to save you from your crimes against God and He did. That's some good stuff right there! The cancellation of hell along with the inheritance of eternal life; *Wow!* You are guaranteed pleasures at God's right hand forevermore[67] because of Jesus! This sounds like a pretty good deal to me—how 'bout you?

It's because God loves you so much Jesus agreed to rescue your soul. Hearing and re-enforcing eternal truth is what grows your faith. Faith comes by hearing the Word of God. Always celebrate the *One* who recreated you to be *One New Dude,* for He is worthy to be praised!

> "For God loved the world so much that he gave his one and only Son, so that everyone who believes in him will not perish but have eternal life."
> **~ John 3:16 NLT**

Why should you change your mind & your life?
Solid Reason #6:
You have One Soul!

Ask, Seek, Knock.
Stop doubting and believe!

Life Application

1. Have you come across anything more important than your soul? Would you sell one of your eyes for a million dollars? If not, then how much more valuable your soul since your eyes are merely the windows of your soul? Have you come to Jesus to find an anchor for your soul?

2. As *One New Dude*, is your life different since you found Jesus as the anchor for your soul? In what ways?

3. Has your understanding and appreciation of the soul compelled you to reach out to other souls—who do not have the anchor of Jesus?

PERSONAL NOTES

Conclusion

Due to the incomprehensible grace of God, you possess every spiritual blessing in Christ God intended for you to possess. Some *mind-blowing* divine transactions took place when Jesus established this new covenant by his precious shed blood.

Remember:
God emphasizes "One"

"There is <u>one</u> body and <u>one</u> Spirit, just as also you were called in <u>one</u> hope of your calling; <u>one</u> Lord, <u>one</u> faith, <u>one</u> baptism, <u>one</u> God and Father of all who is over all and through all and in all."
~ **Ephesians 4:4-6 NASB**

We took—what I would suspect to be—some *seriously* needed inventory! Remaining mindful of the *"7 Solid Reasons to Change your Mind and Life"* can be a terrific source of encouragement for you as you finish out your journey. Those solid reasons are as follows:

You have one new heart. How important is it to have been given a tender *heart of flesh* when a rebellious, stony heart only leads to judgment and eternal separation from a holy and just God? It is indeed *paramount!* This is the heart Christ gave to you. You are only permitted to possess the heart given in the new covenant. You don't get to keep or claim the old, deceitful, wicked and stony heart once you pass *Go* with Jesus. Jesus traded the old one in for you. Mixing covenants is not permitted. Cherish your new heart and above everything, guard it with all diligence!

You have one new mind. No matter how *jacked up* some thoughts which have entered into your mind seem to be, never lose hope. Always stand upon God's Word. It reveals to you without question—you have the mind of Christ. *Turn the key* on this. When you take God at his Word, you ward off the lies of the enemy and grab hold of what God says. If God didn't want your faith to rise to a level where you are actually persuaded of this, the Holy Spirit would have never moved men to write it. As it turns out, you do have this new mind of Christ. When the baited hook of double-mindedness drops, swim by it and feed on God's truth, instead!

You have one nature. Contrary to how you may have been taught or are still being taught, there is no biblical bucket allowing for your sinful nature/old self to exist. Your old nature cannot be both dead and alive. So, you must *turn the key* on this one as well. If you are to experience the *true newness* for which *pure grace* makes provision, you need settle the matter right now if you have yet to do so. In faith, decide once and for all time the *sinful nature is indeed crucified*. God has—why shouldn't you? You *will discover* your true identity when you trust what God says. It may be unchartered waters at first for you, but as you walk in God's truth regarding this matter, He'll renew your mind to a level you otherwise would never have experienced. God is good!

You have one righteousness. Of course, it's not proper English to say, *"one righteousness."* Properly stated it would be something like, *"You have one form or type of righteousness."* This wouldn't fit into the theme of the book, so we had to go a little slang with it. What's most important, though?

No more filthy rags for you, Dude. Christ has imputed his righteousness over to your account. You know, I failed to mention this word-picture earlier. Perhaps you've heard it before, perhaps not. It's that analogy for being justified in God's courtroom, when each of us will stand trial for this life we have lived in the body. Imputed righteousness causes one to be declared innocent even if they were previously guilty. It's a gift. It's grace.

Building upon what was covered in Chapter 5; perhaps a

fitting takeaway for you would be this picture in your mind's eye. Imagine the backroom of a court house where all of the records are kept. Now, imagine the resurrected Christ—nail-pierced hands and perhaps wearing a white robe—reaching directly for the folder with your name on it. In the folder is your R.A.P. sheet, which includes every lie you have ever told, every impure thought you have had, and so on. The list is long and it's actually more like a binder.

Grabbing your *binder,* Jesus takes a very thin folder with his name on it and inserts it where your binder rested. His folder is flawless and impeccable. There's no list of crimes, not even one. He never lied, stole, nor had an impure thought—nothing of the sort. He lived a perfect, sinless life.

When it came for you to be called before Him as the Judge, He was given your file which was actually the file of Jesus Christ. Judgment was in your favor and you were granted eternal bliss in Heaven because of what Christ had done for you. When you trusted Christ to save you, this is what occurred. You were justified: *"just-as-if-I'd-never-sinned."* This is another way to remember it. Jesus imputed his righteousness to you and you can boldly face the Day of Judgment because Jesus has you covered! God's righteousness comes only by grace through faith in Christ's finished work. You've gone from rags to riches, Dude!

You are one spirit. It's the spirit which is the dynamic, inner force within you. Without God's Holy Spirit, you were doomed to a life of sin and condemnation. However, you are enjoying and celebrating the good news of Jesus Christ as *One New Dude!* God's Holy Spirit— united with your spirit as *one spirit*—made you alive in Christ. He has *sealed* you for the day of redemption!

You have one soul. Whether you are a *spirit* who has a soul and a body, or a *soul* who has a spirit and a body, only one thing really matters: Has your soul received atonement? For the born again *One New Dude*, it certainly has received *"at-one-ment"* with God because of the finished work of Christ at Calvary.

According to Jesus, getting this part right is the most reasonable thing a soul can do! I want to encourage you today no matter who you are or what you have been through, all souls are precious to God. Jesus is crazy about you and his arms are stretched wide open to forgive you. As *One New Dude*, you have been forgiven once for all crimes! You can rest assured Christ is the Shepherd of your soul.

"For you were straying like sheep, but have now returned to the Shepherd and Overseer of your souls."
~ 1 Peter 2:25 ESV

You are One New Dude. When you consider all of the things your Heavenly Father has done for you in Christ, it's hard not to get excited, isn't it? Your true identity *is* in Jesus Christ! As Christ is in heaven *so are you in this world.* Not later. Right now… in this world! The *Holy Spirit* is united with *your spirit* as *one spirit*, remember? You live—*yet not you*—but *Christ in you* lives! Receive it. God said it. Heaven and earth will pass away but God's Word lasts for how long? Forever!

"Put on then, as God's chosen ones, holy and beloved, compassionate hearts, kindness, humility, meekness, and patience, bearing with one another and, if one has a complaint against another, forgiving each other; as the Lord has forgiven you, so you also must forgive. And above all these put on love, which binds everything together in perfect harmony."
~ Colossians 3:12-14 ESV

Why should you change your mind & your life?
Solid Reason #7:
You are
One New Dude!

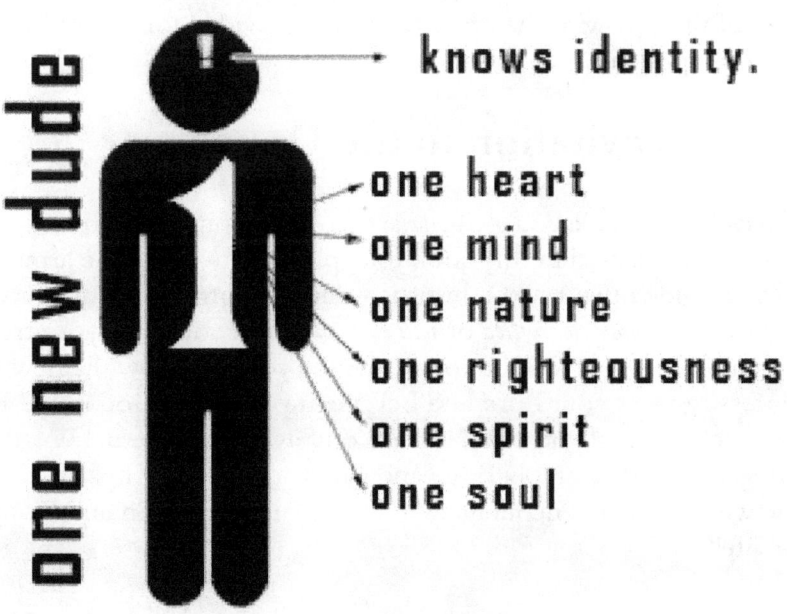

Ask, Seek, Knock.
Stop doubting and believe!

Invitation to the Believer

If you are a Christian who has suffered from a fractured identity—Jesus invites you right now to *turn the key!* Never again believe the lie you share space with the *old you*. God has re-created you and you are an entirely new creature! Old things have passed away according to the truth of God. Therefore, receive God's grace through faith in Jesus Christ entirely. Don't settle for going part of the way. Rather, go all of the way with the grace Jesus has provided for you as his blood-bought child!

Invitation to the Unbeliever

If Jesus hasn't made you a Christian yet—but you are interested for the truths presented in this book to apply to you—then the arms of Jesus are wide open to you. Jesus is willing to forgive you of every single sin you *have committed* or *will ever commit*. If you place your trust in Him by *calling out* to Him today, the old you *will become* the new you. Confess Jesus as your Lord and believe in your heart God raised Him from the dead and you *will be saved*. You have God's eternal Word on it! Begin to read the Holy Bible and get around other Christ-Followers who can encourage you in your new direction and brand new life!

JESUS SPEAKS: "The kingdom of heaven is like treasure hidden in a field. When a man found it, he hid it again, and then in his joy went and sold all he had and bought that field."
~ Matthew 13:44 NIV

If this book has been helpful to you, please consider leaving a review on this book's Amazon page.

#1: Be sure to: register for blog updates and get other titles of this book @:
www.**NoWayDude.org**

#2: Read over and be encouraged by the much anticipated Foundation of this series:
"NO WAY DUDE" – How You Got To Heaven

Be sure to share with unsaved loved ones, friends, colleagues and the world. Let **"NO WAY DUDE"** do the work of explaining the Gospel for you!

Resources & Links

Suggested Reading

Amazon.com

1. *Freedom From Sin*, John MacArthur
2. *Destined to Reign*, Joseph Prince
3. *Classic Christianity*, Bob George
4. *The School of the Seers,* Jonathan Welton
5. *Eyes of Honor*, Jonathan Welton
6. *Tactics*, Greg Koukl

Suggested Audio

Freedom from Sin, John MacArthur, gty.org
http://www.gty.org/resources/sermon-series/153

Suggested Links

1. No Way Dude, nowaydude.org
2. Grace to You, gty.org
3. Joseph Prince, josephprince.com
4. Power and Love, powerandlove.org
5. Stand to Reason, str.org

About Jeff Zahorsky

Jeff Zahorsky was born in 1968 in Cleveland, Ohio to Irish and Slovak parents. A veteran of the United States Navy, Jeff served just over 6 years, primarily on Navy warships with one ground tour in Iraq. With technology as his background, Jeff holds a Certificate of Biomedicine from Boston University. It was on the flight deck of a U.S. Navy warship in Pearl Harbor, HI where he became a Christian. Jeff aspires in sharing God's eternal truth through his ongoing writings.

Stay connected via:
www.NoWayDude.org

Endnotes

1 John 5:6
2 Jonathan Welton, *The School of the Seers*, (Shippensburg, PA: Destiny Image, 2009)
3 *"What is the Heart?,"* gotquestions.org, http://www.gotquestions.org/what-is-the-heart.html (accessed 11/1/12)
4 Jonathan Welton, *"True Identity",* http://www.youtube.com/watch?v=Bq4OGJJWiEE (accessed 6/25/12)
5 Jeremiah 17:9
6 *"What is the Heart?,"* gotquestions.org, http://www.gotquestions.org/what-is-the-heart.html (accessed 11/1/12)
7 Jeremiah 32:27
8 *"Be transformed"* — *more than a costume party"*, Wolfgang Schneider, http://www.biblecenter.de/bibel/studien/e-std029.php (accessed 10/28/12)
9 "How can I have the mind of Christ?," gotquestions.org, http://www.gotquestions.org/mind-of-Christ.html (accessed 11/1/12)
10 Jonathan Welton, *"True Identity",* http://www.youtube.com/watch?v=Bq4OGJJWiEE (accessed 6/25/12)
11 Romans 8:7
12 John MacArthur, *Freedom From Sin* (Chicago, IL: Moody Press, September 1987), 172.
13 Blue Letter Bible. "Dictionary and Word Search for pisteuō (Strong's 4100)". Blue Letter Bible. 1996-2012. 20 Nov 2012. < http://www.blueletterbible.org/lang/lexicon/Lexicon.cfm?strongs=G4100 > (accessed 10/19/2012)
14 Jonathan Welton, *The School of the Seers*, (Shippensburg, PA: Destiny Image, 2009)
15 Luke 14:28
16 Matthew 12:30 NASB
17 Luke 9:62 NLT
18 Blue Letter Bible. "Dictionary and Word Search for physis (Strong's 5449)". Blue Letter Bible. 1996-2012. 20 Nov 2012. < http://www.blueletterbible.org/lang/lexicon/Lexicon.cfm?strongs=G5449 >
19 Blue Letter Bible. "Dictionary and Word Search for dynamis (Strong's 1411)". Blue Letter Bible. 1996-2012. 20 Nov 2012. < http://www.blueletterbible.org/lang/lexicon/Lexicon.cfm?strongs=G1411 >

20 Luke 1:41
21 Psalms 51:5
22 Romans 10:17
23 Galatians 5:24
24 BibleTools.org, *"Oil as Symbol,"* http://www.bibletools.org/index.cfm/fuseaction/Topical.show/RTD/cg/ID/1107/Oil-as-Symbol.htm (accessed 11/20/2012)
25 Joseph Prince, *Destined to Reign*, (Tulsa, OK: Harrison House Publishers, January 25, 2010)
26 Hebrews 10:22
27 Romans 6:18
28 Blue Letter Bible. "Dictionary and Word Search for sarx (Strong's 4561)". Blue Letter Bible. 1996-2012. 20 Nov 2012. < http://www.blueletterbible.org/lang/lexicon/Lexicon.cfm?strongs=G4561 > (accessed 10/19/12)
29 John MacArthur, *Freedom from Sin* (Chicago, IL: Moody Press, September 1987), 173.
30 John MacArthur, *Freedom from Sin* (Chicago, IL: Moody Press, September 1987), 112.
31 John MacArthur, *Freedom from Sin* (Chicago, IL: Moody Press, September 1987), 111.
32 *"Freedom From Sin,"* http://www.gty.org/resources/positions/P13/freedom-from-sin (accessed:10/19/2012)
33 Grace to You, *"Freedom From Sin,"* http://www.gty.org/resources/positions/P13/freedom-from-sin (accessed:10/19/2012)
34 Psalms 115:3
35 Janice Seney, *"Body, Soul, Spirit,"* http://www.youtube.com/watch?v=HqO5JFEldmc (accessed:10/15/2012)
36 Romans 1-8, MacArthur New Testament Commentary, p. 326
37 John MacArthur, *Freedom from Sin* (Chicago, IL: Moody Press, September 1987), 173.
38 Bill Johnson, *"Identify the Devil's Lie,"* http://www.youtube.com/watch?v=psx-iP56JiE&feature=related (accessed 10/10/2012)
39 Jonathan Welton, *"True Identity",* http://www.youtube.com/watch?v=Bq4OGJJWiEE (accessed 6/25/12)
40 Numbers 23:19
41 Romans 8:1
42 Ephesians 5:26
43 John 8:44
44 Romans 8:29
45 *"What is progressive sanctification?,"* gotquestions.org, http://www.gotquestions.org/progressive-sanctification.html (accessed 10/18/12)

46 Hebrews 10:14
47 *"How Long Does a Butterfly Stay in a Chrysalis Cocoon?,"* http://www.ehow.com/about_4572522_does-butterfly-stay-chrysalis-cocoon.html (accessed 10/1/12)
48 Romans 6:3
49 Jonathan Welton, *"True Identity",* http://www.youtube.com/watch?v=Bq4OGJJWiEE (accessed 6/25/12)
50 Proverbs 28:1
51 Matthew 4:4
52 Montell Jordan, *"F.L.H.,"* http://www.youtube.com/watch?v=Hxc76U-cciw (accessed 6/28/12)
53 Matthew 28:18 NASB
54 Grace to You, *"Freedom From Sin,"* http://www.gty.org/resources/positions/P13/freedom-from-sin (accessed:10/19/2012)
55 Matthew 10:16
56 *"What Are All the Life Cycle Stages for the Locust Cicada?,"* http://www.ehow.com/info_8575763_life-cycle-stages-locust-cicada.html (accessed 10/17/12)
57 *"What is righteousness?,"* gotquestions.org, http://www.gotquestions.org/righteousness.html (accessed 11/10/12)
58 *"Why does Christ's righteousness need to be imputed to us?,"* gotquestions.org, http://www.gotquestions.org/imputed-righteousness.html (accessed 11/10/12)
59 Todd White
60 "What is the human spirit?," gotquestions.org, http://www.gotquestions.org/human-spirit.html (accessed 11/5/12)
61 Blue Letter Bible. "Dictionary and Word Search for něshamah (Strong's 5397)". Blue Letter Bible. 1996-2012. 20 Nov 2012. < http://www.blueletterbible.org/lang/lexicon/Lexicon.cfm?strongs=H5397 >
62 Blue Letter Bible. "Dictionary and Word Search for pneuma (Strong's 4151)". Blue Letter Bible. 1996-2012. 20 Nov 2012. < http://www.blueletterbible.org/lang/lexicon/Lexicon.cfm?strongs=G4151 >
63 *"What is the human soul?,"* gotquestions.org, http://www.gotquestions.org/human-soul.html (accessed 11/5/12)
64 Janice Seney, *"Body, Soul, Spirit"* http://www.youtube.com/watch?feature=endscreen&v=FTy9mjVHYSw&NR=1 (accessed 9/15/12)
65 *"What is the human soul?,"* gotquestions.org, http://www.gotquestions.org/human-soul.html (accessed 11/5/12)
66 Psalms 139:14

[67] Psalms 16:11

www.ingramcontent.com/pod-product-compliance
Lightning Source LLC
Chambersburg PA
CBHW061642040426
42446CB00010B/1541